Women Who Encountered Jesus

WOMEN
WHO ENCOUNTERED
JESUS

Faye Field

BROADMAN PRESS
Nashville, Tennessee

4251-82
ISBN: 0-8054-5182

Dewey Decimal Classification: 225.92
Subject heading: WOMEN IN THE BIBLE
Library of Congress Catalog Card Number: 81-65798
Printed in the United States of America

Preface

There are eighteen occasions on which Jesus spoke to women. However, there are only twelve women for whom we have direct, personal conversations recorded. There was the brief answer to a woman crying out in the crowd; a like brief statement to the weeping women as Jesus was on his way to Calvary. Then on resurrection day there were indefinite references to several women, differing according to the Gospel writers. There seems to have been a statement made to the other Mary (mother of James), Salome, Joanna, and other women.

Jesus spoke to his mother on three separate occasions as recorded in the Gospels. He also spoke to Martha on two occasions, as recorded.

Thus, if we take away the three general references to conversations and the three times he talked with the same women, we have "the chosen twelve" women left with whom Jesus had conversations more or less in detail.

These women seem to represent twelve categories of women to whom the message of Jesus is significant in any age, even today. The categories are: mothers concerned with children, those in conflict over good and evil desires, those experiencing loss of loved ones, those who have values that others criticize, those involved in physical suffering, those who are dead in spirit, those who have to plead for others, those who are caught in sin, those who are encumbered over trivial matters, those who are deformed or handicapped, those who are ambitious for recognition and prominence, and those who are not quite ready for miracles.

Contents

1. Mary, the Mother of Jesus   9
2. The Woman of Samaria   19
3. The Widow of Nain   33
4. The Woman Who Anointed
   Jesus' Feet   41
5. The Woman with an Issue of Blood   51
6. The Daughter of Jairus   59
7. The Syrophenician Woman   69
8. The Woman Taken in Adultery   79
9. Martha   89
10. The Woman with a Spirit of
    Infirmity   101
11. Salome—Mother of James and John   109
12. Mary Magdalene   119

1

Mary, the Mother of Jesus

A Mother Who Pondered

Luke 2:41-52

Now his parents went to Jerusalem every year at the feast of the passover.

And when he was twelve years old, they went up to Jerusalem after the custom of the feast.

And when they had fulfilled the days, as they returned, the child Jesus tarried behind in Jerusalem; and Joseph and his mother knew not of it.

But they, supposing him to have been in the company, went a day's journey; and they sought him among their kinsfolk and acquaintance.

And when they found him not, they turned back again to Jerusalem, seeking him.

And it came to pass, that after three days they found him in the temple, sitting in the midst of the doctors, both hearing them, and asking them questions.

And all that heard him were astonished at his understanding and answers.

And when they saw him, they were amazed: and his mother said unto him, Son, why hast thou dealt thus with us? behold, thy father and I have sought thee sorrowing.

And he said unto them, How is it that ye sought me?

wist ye not that I must be about my Father's business?

And they understood not the saying which he spake unto them.

And he went down with them, and came to Nazareth, and was subject unto them: but his mother kept all these sayings in her heart.

And Jesus increased in wisdom and stature, and in favour with God and man.

This scene took place during the period of preparation in the early life of Jesus. This is the only mention made of Jesus from his infancy until he began his ministry. No other Gospel writer tells of this incident.

His parents had gone to Jerusalem as they did every year for the Feast of the Passover. This feast was the greatest of the three feasts which males were compelled to attend. The other two feasts were the Feast of Pentecost and the Feast of Tabernacles. Joseph, of course, attended all of these feasts, but Mary went only to the Passover feast.

Now, Jesus was with them at the Passover feast. He was twelve years old, the age at which Jewish boys began to fast. It was also at the age of twelve that a boy was called "son of the law," and first incurred legal obligations.

The family had a long journey to make to Jerusalem, and they were poor, but the feast of the Passover could not be missed. They were required to stay at the feast for two days, but it seems that Joseph, Mary, and Jesus may have stayed the full seven days of the feast.

Now as the parents were returning, Jesus remained in Jerusalem. Mary and Joseph were not aware of this, for they supposed that he was in the company of other young people.

It may have taken quite a while to look through the company searching for him since a great caravan of people made the journey to Jerusalem.

After three days—perhaps one in travel, one in searching for Jesus, and one in returning—they found Jesus back in the Temple in the midst of the learned doctors there.

Out of their amazement came Mary's question, "Why?"

Now we hear the first recorded words of Jesus, "How is it that ye sought me? wist ye not that I must be about my Father's business?"

His response was gentle but prophetic.

They were not able to understand what he said, but as they went back to Nazareth, Mary pondered on his words.

Perhaps they became more meaningful to her as she saw Jesus increase in wisdom, and stature, and in favor with God and man.

We do not need to conjecture about why Jesus chose his mother as one of the twelve women with whom he would speak. We have records that the Lord spoke to her twice more. He would of necessity place a verbal bond between himself and his mother who would love so much and have so much joy and so much sorrow to experience through him.

What women of today belong in this group with Mary? It is all the women who seek their sons, and then upon finding them, do not understand what they are doing or what they are saying.

To these modern women, Jesus would perhaps say again, "Wist not"—and they, too, must ponder these sayings in their hearts.

A Mother Who Felt Her Son's Purpose

John 2:1-12

And the third day there was a marriage in Cana of Galilee; and the mother of Jesus was there:

And both Jesus was called, and his disciples, to the marriage.

And when they wanted wine, the mother of Jesus saith unto him, They have no wine.

Jesus saith unto her, Woman, what have I to do with thee? mine hour is not yet come.

His mother saith unto the servants, Whatsoever he saith unto you, do it.

And there were set there six waterpots of stone, after the manner of the purifying of the Jews, containing two or three firkins apiece.

Jesus saith unto them, Fill the waterpots with water. And they filled them up to the brim.

And he saith unto them, Draw out now, and bear unto the governor of the feast. And they bare it.

When the ruler of the feast had tasted the water that was made wine, and knew not whence it was: (but the servants which drew the water knew;) the governor of the feast called the bridegroom,

And saith unto him, Every man at the beginning doth set forth good wine; and when men have well drunk, then that which is worse: but thou hast kept the good wine until now.

This beginning of miracles did Jesus in Cana of Galilee, and manifested forth his glory; and his disciples believed on him.

John is the only Gospel writer who records this miracle. It may be that he was there and witnessed this miracle, or Mary, the mother of Jesus, may have told him about this after he took her to his home to live with him.

This miracle occurred right after Jesus' victory over Satan in the wilderness. It took place in the opening events of Jesus' ministry; in fact, it was the first miracle that Jesus performed. The place was Cana which was only a few miles from Nazareth. Cana was settled by the tribe of Asher. Here was where Nathanael, one of the disciples called by Jesus very early in his ministry, lived.

There was a wedding at Cana; Jesus and his disciples had been invited. His idsciples were at the time: John, Peter, Andrew, Philip, and Nathanael. Jesus' presence here signifies his respect for marriage as a divine institution.

Now an embarrassing situation developed. The hosts ran out of wine. It was the custom for guests to bring wine to a wedding feast as a present. It may be that Jesus and his disciples did not bring wine. Maybe this is what caused the shortage of refreshments. If this were the case, maybe this is why Mary brought the problem to Jesus. It seems that this wedding was being held in the home of a relative of Mary's, or else Mary would not have been so ready to assume authority.

Mary's seeking out Jesus showed that she had sympathy for her hosts' embarrassment.

When Mary told Jesus that they had no wine, we are not sure of her thoughts. Maybe she had the knowledge of his power in her heart. No one knew Jesus as she did. She may have thought about the shepherds, the Wise Men, the day in the Temple when he was twelve years old. She may have already heard about the things that had happened recently at the Jordan—John the Baptist baptizing Jesus, the calling of Philip, and what Jesus had said he knew about Nathanael. Maybe Mary was seeking a sign from Jesus.

When Jesus answered her, he called her "Woman," not "Mother." This is not a harsh word but rather a token of respect. It is the same tender word that he used at the cross when he spoke to her. Perhaps he used the word woman instead of mother to show her that her maternal authority was at an end.

Jesus seemed to consider his mother as interfering with God's will as he said, "What have I to do with thee? mine hour is not yet come."

His words seem to mean, "Don't interfere," but they may have just as well meant, "Don't worry."

Mary kept a quiet confidence in him. She made no reply to what may have been a reproof. Like the Syrophenician woman—out of a rebuff, she made another plea. For Mary went right on telling the servants to do whatever he told them to do.

Nothing is said of Joseph in this story. Perhaps he was already dead at that time.

Mary withdrew from the center of the scene. Jesus performed the miracle by having the servants fill the waterpots, and the water was made wine—the finest wine they had.

This miracle seems to be the frontispiece of the Gospel of John.

This miracle shows that Christ enriches everything for us. Jesus' first miracle brought joy. It also demonstrates that the relationship between Mary and Jesus had changed. She was not again in the forefront until at the cross.

Again we are not amazed that Jesus chose to speak to his mother again. It would be a puzzle if he had not spoken to her more frequently than he did to the other women.

What group of modern women belong with Mary in this particular scene of the first miracle? All women of today belong in this category who have confidence in their sons because of what they know about their sons' upbringing, who have seen their sons going out to do greater things than they ever dreamed of, who gracefully withdraw from the center of the scene as their sons come to prominence. These mothers also accept a new relationship with their sons in this adjustment. Hopefully, modern women of this group, accepting change as well as Mary did, will later, like her, come back into more significance in the lives of their sons.

A Mother Taken Care Of

John 19:25-27

Now there stood by the cross of Jesus his mother, and his mother's sister, Mary the wife of Cleophas, and Mary Magdalene.

When Jesus therefore saw his mother, and the disciple standing by, whom he loved, he saith unto his mother, Woman, behold thy son!

Then saith he unto the disciple, Behold thy mother! And from that hour that disciple took her unto his own home.

The last time Jesus spoke to his mother, as far as we know, was from the cross.

She must have been near the foot of the cross as Jesus spoke those words. Perhaps later the soldiers made them move away. She stood there with Mary, the wife of Cleophas; Mary Magdalene; and we think the fourth woman standing there was Salome.

The Scriptures describe Mary as standing there composed. She was not tearing her hair, rending her clothes, or screaming.

Now Jesus confirmed the relationship with his beloved mother and his beloved disciple.

He perhaps used the word *Woman,* when he told her to behold her son, to hurt her less.

Jesus, in taking care of his mother in that manner, revealed that when God takes away one comfort, he provides another.

Jesus conferred an honor upon John when he said, "Behold thy mother!"

It is strange that Mary's presence at the cross is recorded by no other Gospel writer. Even on the cross Jesus planned for others.

His address to his mother was not rude but was formal. The word *Woman* may even have had a hidden meaning that we are not aware of fully.

There is no other mention made of Mary during that last week in the life of Jesus. Maybe she took her cue from what Jesus said at the wedding in Cana when he performed his first miracle. She may have followed his wishes by staying in the background.

Jesus' last bequest was to his mother and to John. It was all the wealth he had. We are told that from that very hour John took Mary to his home. Her name is mentioned only once more, in the Book of Acts.

In this scene Jesus reached out to his mother *with John's arms.*

Maybe Jesus called his mother "woman" to indicate his sorrow for all grieving womanhood. It is comforting for women to know that Jesus' last act was to take care of his mother.

Jesus, of course, wanted to speak to his mother a third time, his last time. This would be the last women he addressed before his death. This last speaking to his mother sanctified their relationship.

Which women belong in this group today?

All women who stand sorrowing as their sons are about to depart this life.

The message of Christ is the same today to these bereaved women as it was to Mary at the cross:

First, that their love of Christ will fit them to carry on his tasks.

Second, that the healing for sorrow is taking on new relationships, new responsibilities, new patterns.

Third, there is comfort and strength in sharing.

Fourth, whatever fills the empty places of life, is divine comfort!

2

The Woman of Samaria

The Woman in Whom Good and Evil Met

John 4:4-30,39-42

And he must needs go through Samaria.

Then cometh he to a city of Samaria, which is called Sychar, near to the parcel of ground that Jacob gave to his son Joseph.

Now Jacob's well was there. Jesus therefore, being wearied with his journey, sat thus on the well: and it was about the sixth hour.

There cometh a woman of Samaria to draw water: Jesus saith unto her, Give me to drink.

(For his disciples were gone away unto the city to buy meat.)

Then saith the woman of Samaria unto him, How is it that thou, being a Jew, askest drink of me, which am a woman of Samaria? for the Jews have no dealings with the Samaritans.

Jesus answered and said unto her, If thou knewest the gift of God, and who it is that saith to thee, Give me to drink; thou wouldest have asked of him, and he would have given thee living water.

The woman saith unto him, Sir, thou hast nothing to draw with, and the well is deep: from whence then hast thou that living water?

Art thou greater than our father Jacob, which gave

19

us the well, and drank thereof himself, and his children, and his cattle?

Jesus answered and said unto her, Whosoever drinketh of this water shall thirst again:

But whosoever drinketh of the water that I shall give him shall never thirst; but the water that I shall give him shall be in him a well of water springing up into everlasting life.

The woman saith unto him, Sir, give me this water, that I thirst not, neither come hither to draw.

Jesus saith unto her, Go, call thy husband, and come hither.

The woman answered and said, I have no husband. Jesus said unto her, Thou hast well said, I have no husband:

For thou hast had five husbands; and he whom thou now hast is not thy husband: in that saidst thou truly.

The woman saith unto him, Sir, I perceive that thou art a prophet.

Our fathers worshipped in this mountain; and ye say, that in Jerusalem is the place where men ought to worship.

Jesus saith unto her, Woman, believe me, the hour cometh, when ye shall neither in this mountain, nor yet at Jerusalem, worship the Father.

Ye worship ye know not what: we know what we worship: for salvation is of the Jews.

But the hour cometh, and now is, when the true worshippers shall worship the Father in spirit and in truth: for the Father seeketh such to worship him.

God is a Spirit: and they that worship him must worship him in spirit and in truth.

The woman saith unto him, I know that Messias cometh, which is called Christ: when he is come, he will tell us all things.

Jesus saith unto her, I that speak unto thee am he.

And upon this came his disciples, and marvelled that he talked with the woman: yet no man said, What seekest thou? or, Why talkest thou with her?

The woman then left her waterpot, and went her way into the city, and saith to the men,

Come, see a man, which told me all things that ever I did: is not this the Christ?

Then they went out of the city, and came unto him.
. . . .

And many of the Samaritans of that city believed on him for the saying of the woman, which testified, He told me all that ever I did.

So when the Samaritans were come unto him, they besought him that he would tarry with them: and he abode there two days.

And many more believed because of his own word;

And said unto the woman, Now we believe, not because of thy saying: for we have heard him ourselves, and know that this is indeed the Christ, the Saviour of the world.

How did Jesus come to talk with this woman of Samaria?

Let's look at the circumstances.

The need was there. The journey was far from pleasant in this hostile land. Most Jewish travelers took the longer route through Perea in going from Judea to Galilee. But the need for Jesus to travel this particular shorter way was imperative.

So Jesus arrived at the ground which was historic for both the Jews and the Samaritans. The prophets Elijah, Elisha, and Hosea had labored there. Jacob, along with Joseph and his brothers, had been familiar figures there.

Now, Jesus, sitting on Jacob's well, affords one of the few scenes where we find him alone. His disciples have gone into the city to buy meat.

Then at the sixth hour came a woman of Samaria to draw water.

Mystery surrounds her. Why did she show up alone instead of with a group of women as was the custom in that time? Why did she come at the hottest time of the day, at the noon hour?

Jesus was so weary that even his manner of sitting indicated his fatigue. Yet he seized the opportunity to help this poor woman. In his ministry to her he gives us the lesson that every soul is valuable.

He had the utmost tact by putting her at ease when he began the conversation by asking a favor of her. Too, he may have wished to arouse her sympathy and concern as she saw him worn and thirsty. The question he asked was common enough. Travel-worn sojourners often asked for water from the women drawing from the wells along the road.

Next we view the quickness of the woman's mind and also the puzzlement as she asked why he would seek a favor from a member of a hated hybrid race. She answered his request with her own question.

Jesus did not answer her question directly. He did not talk of the dispute between Jews and Samaritans. He rather sought the opportunity to elevate her to a higher concept of life. We learn from his method that some differences are better left without discussion.

There are seven outstanding statements which Jesus uttered in the conversation with this woman of Samaria. Perhaps one of the most pivotal of these communications was his second warning, "If thou knewest the gift of God."

The woman's reaction to this statement revealed her as one who was eager to learn. Her curiosity was aroused by the reference Jesus made to "living water."

We do not know how much of the philosophy of Jesus she understood, but certainly enough to merit her respect for Jesus. Her second response began with the appellation, "Sir," a title of dignity.

Jesus spoke figuratively—she took his words literally.

We know that she was deeply aware of her heritage as she spoke of Jacob and his family. We see that she had a logical mind as she sought to identify Jesus through comparison with the ancient patriarchs.

In the third statement Jesus made he described in detail the spiritual offering he was making to her. He explained that what is done by human hands cannot satisfy permanently. Perhaps he was referring to those who had turned against her. He countered this burden by advising her of a "well" within.

Maybe the words, "never thirst," literally made a sensitive appeal to this woman. *What a comfort,* she may have thought, *never again to have to do the menial labor of drawing water from the deep well.* Also she may have grasped the figurative appeal, for she apparently thirsted for so many, many things. She needed companionship, peace of mind, acceptance, rest, security of a home, and just about everything a destitute person counted as lost forever.

When she asked Jesus to give her this water, we are not sure if she said this in jest or in earnest.

In the fourth statement, "Go, call thy husband," Jesus used the utmost concern in appealing to her sense of sin. He was bringing sharply into focus the necessity of repentance before she could have the gift of living water. It followed that she had to face the need, confess her sins, turn to Jesus, and then expect the gift to be bestowed. How wonderful to realize that God's gift is living water! Jesus made it quite clear that her heart must be pricked in order for her to hear in truth.

Perhaps the greatest hope and expectation for the outcome of the conversation was when she answered in simple honesty, "I have no husband."

Jesus had given her the motive for falsehood, but she chose to speak the truth, regardless of the consequences.

The fifth time Jesus addressed her he commended her for her truthfulness. Then he hastened to add a brief description of the way she had lived in sin, accurately describing her situation.

In complimenting her truthfulness, Jesus picked out the most commendable thing about her. Even then as he told of her sordid past, he used words that were mild, not provoking.

It is remarkable that this discourse could continue even after her faults had been aired. Her humility was revealed in the fact that she was not angered by Jesus' accusation of her. Instead she gained insight enough to declare that he must be a prophet.

However, she was evidently embarrassed, for she tried to turn the conversation, which had been so soul-searching of her sins, into a theological discussion. She wanted to know where the proper site for true worship was— was it in the Temple in Jerusalem or was it on Mount Gerizim?

Still, she may have actually longed to know where she could pray for this gift—of living water so much under discussion.

The sixth time Jesus spoke he began with a note of tenderness. He called her "Woman." This is the same appellation he used in talking with his mother in John 2:4 at the wedding feast in Cana.

This next-to-the-last statement Jesus made to the woman centered around the basic concept, "God is a spirit." Surely Jesus was conveying the truth that the highest part of humankind's nature is attuned to God.

In this discussion Jesus resolved her doubt about where she needed to worship. How wonderfully Jesus explained that one's religion should not stand between one and God! Thus, a good person is satisfied from within himself, for Christ dwells in his heart.

The woman is seen as having a beginning faith, as she said, "I know that Messias cometh."

The final announcement that Jesus made was a disclosure of himself.

"I that speak unto thee am he."

This is the first public disclosure that Jesus made. Never did he make himself more expressly known than to this poor Samaritan woman standing there in the noonday sun! She had wasted her best years. Though coming late, she now stood in his presence! She probably never had witnessed any of his miracles that he had performed in Judea, Galilee, or Perea. But now she knew who he was!

There was an interrupting interval. The disciples returned from the city with the food for Jesus. They were amazed when they saw Jesus talking to the woman. This scene broke the tradition of talking to a woman in public, especially a rabbi engaged thus. Yet the disciples remained silent, not daring to ask Jesus about the strange happenings.

After the woman left the scene, Jesus, thinking perhaps of his influence upon the woman, urged his disciples to "look on the fields ripe unto harvest."

We do not understand why the woman left from the well so hurriedly. She may have been embarrassed or even fearful at the sight of the group of men approaching. On the other hand, she may have been excited, and like a happy child, ran to tell the good news that she had seen the Christ. She could have left through courtesy so Jesus could go ahead and eat the food his disciples had brought in.

In her haste, she left the waterpot. She evidently forgot all about her errand in the compelling power of her marvelous discovery. However, she could have left the waterpot for Jesus so the water could be drawn from the well to go with the food then ready for him.

She did not let the past close her lips. We are told that many of the Samaritans of that city believed on him for the saying of the woman. Many came out of the city to meet Jesus.

So, in receiving the gift, one good work applied to another as she ran to tell her neighbors. Christ told her to call her husband, but she went to call *everybody.*

She became, in a sense, an apostle!

One poor woman spread instruction to a whole town. What a change she helped bring about! Those Samaritans, who formerly didn't even want Jesus to pass through their land, now begged him to stay with them. So urgently did they seek him that he stayed there two days longer.

Now the question is—how does the conversation of Jesus with the woman at the well affect women of today?

First of all, why was this woman of Samaria one of the chosen twelve women whom Jesus singled out from all the myriads of women of that day? Why did he choose to speak directly to her?

Let us examine some of the characteristics of this singular woman, even though the encounter with Jesus was brief.

We learn right away that she must have been poor. She had no servant to draw the water for her.

The next fact about her is that she must have been very frightened or very resentful of those she would encounter at the well. Otherwise, she would not have come at the sixth hour of the day for this hard task.

No doubt she was living in sin. She had lived with five husbands and the man she was living with at the time was not her husband.

The Scriptures reveal that she had an inquiring mind, for she asked, "How is it?"

We know that she was well aware of racial prejudice.

She was respectful of authority. She addressed Jesus as "Sir."

She possessed logical reasoning as she said, "Thou hast nothing to draw with." She had reverence for her heritage as she recalled the habits of the patriarchs.

She was seeking improvement as she said, "Give me this water."

She possessed truthfulness as she replied without regard to the consequences, "I have no husband." She was perceptive, for she readily recognized Jesus as a prophet.

She was clever, for she tried to change the subject of the conversation when Jesus accused her. She believed the Scriptures when she said, "The Messias is coming."

She must have been a courteous person, for she left her waterpot so Jesus could have drink with his food. She was able to return good for evil. She went back to share Christ with the people who had taunted her. She was effective in proclaiming Christ, and many came to believe on him.

When we examine the latent possibilities for good in this woman, it is no wonder that Jesus singled her out for conversation.

Into what category does this woman fall? Where is her counterpart in today's womanhood?

We see the woman at the well in many women today. She represents the field of conflict between good and evil. The battle of emotions frustrates perhaps more than ever before the hurts of modern women. Never have there been more pressures on women than at this present time with changing life-styles, different mores, and alternative philosophies.

In this land of plenty, where so many women have servants to do their work for them, it is galling to some women that they must engage in menial labor.

Thousands of women have the haunting insecurity and the hurt pride that results from several marriages having been dissolved. There are "trial marriages," without the sanctity of vows, that women have to deal with in some manner today for the easing of their consciences. No matter how common this practice of living together before marriage has become, the participants still face the resentment of many in this radical life-style.

There are today, like in Jesus' time, women who live on the back streets. They cannot mingle at any hour or at any place they choose because of the fear of meeting their lover's family or friends.

Often these women who have chosen an uneasy way of life, like the woman at the well, possess inquiring minds. Many women today live in the midst of racial prejudice.

Likewise, many women today, whose lives have become entangled in immorality, are deeply respectful of those they admire who have mastered the art of living.

Although modern women who have fouled up their lives in sinful living seem void of logic in this respect, we have evidence that they have logical reasoning in other areas. Often these same women have successful careers and engage in many civic duties.

And there are sinful women who still have a grateful feeling for their Christian heritage from which they have departed.

The increase in marriage-counseling facilities shows that modern women, like their ancient sister, are seeking improvement.

Many modern women do not try to hide the fact that they have live-in partners. They are truthful about their relationships. Modern women are perceptive and clever in handling their precarious situations.

Most women would like to believe the Scriptures, even if they don't live according to the precepts prescribed in the holy Word.

The women of today—caught in this same mire of the woman at the well—when Jesus speaks to them, will also change dramatically. They too will become courteous. They will return good for evil to their tormentors. They will become effective in spreading the good news.

So from the conversation of Jesus with the woman at the well, women today can know him also!

Women in New York City or women out in the boondocks alike can know that Jesus left for all women, bowed down in the field of conflict between good and evil, hope and love.

These tortured ones can rest in the knowledge that One can come to them even after a long period of wasted years. They can also realize that Jesus taught there is in every woman an insatiable longing for fellowship with God. These women can exult in the truth that the lesson of tolerance was the first public teaching of Christ.

There is comfort for these troubled women to recognize that, although on many occasions Jesus preached to thronging multitudes, he took time to reveal himself on a one-to-one basis to the poor, sinful woman in Samaria!

Women of today, are you in this particular category?

Remember that Jesus says to you, "I that speak unto thee am he."

That makes all the difference!

3

The Widow of Nain

The Woman Who Stopped Jesus

Luke 7:11-17

And it came to pass the day after, that he went into a city called Nain; and many of his disciples went with him, and much people.

Now when he came nigh to the gate of the city, behold, there was a dead man carried out, the only son of his mother, and she was a widow: and much people of the city was with her.

And when the Lord saw her, he had compassion on her, and said unto her, Weep not.

And he came and touched the bier: and they that bare him stood still. And he said, Young man, I say unto thee, Arise.

And he that was dead sat up, and began to speak. And he delivered him to his mother.

And there came a fear on all: and they glorified God, saying, That a great prophet is risen up among us; and, That God hath visited his people.

And this rumour of him went forth throughout all Judaea, and throughout all the region round about.

The first of the seemingly greatest miracles that Jesus performed, the raising of the dead, took place around this unnamed woman.

This miracle occurred during the Galilean ministry of Jesus. It was the day after he had left Capernaum where he had healed the centurion's servant.

This miracle happened in a town called Nain. This town is just off one of the roads leading from the lake to the coast on the side of a steep hill. It is mentioned nowhere else in the Bible. It is not far from Capernaum, about four miles south of Mount Tabor. It is not far from Endor and about two and one-half leagues from Nazareth. It was inhabited by only a few families. They were from the tribe of Issachar. The name Nain means "lovely." Perhaps it was so called because of the plain of Esdraelon. The fact that this was such a small place teaches us that the Lord passes over no city with his grace.

Jesus' disciples were with him. They had been especially consecrated the day before for their service. Coming so soon after this dedication, this miracle would serve to strengthen their faith.

Luke twice uses the expression "much people" in this brief story. Some of these people had perhaps heard the Sermon on the Mount. Now they could see that Jesus was acting out his words; "Be merciful as your Father is merciful."

As Jesus came down the main road, he would be facing the big gate of the town, for there was no other entrance to the city. Out of this gate came the funeral procession. The custom of the Jews was to bury immediately after death. The body would be wrapped in linen clothes and then would be carried from the house on a bier. In this instance the graves were cut out of rocks outside the walls of the town. That's why the funeral procession was passing through the gate.

There were two groups present—the disciples, along with other followers of Jesus, and the mourners. Some may think the meeting of these two groups was coincidental, but it was surely the providence of God. This was nothing casual, for all worked together for the glory of God. These were certainly two opposite groups. One moved joyfully, while the other made its way in sorrow.

Two facts make this woman's sorrow particularly hard to bear. She was a widow and this was her only son. Not only would she be left alone without means of livelihood, but for a Jewish woman not to have a son was a grief beyond our comprehension.

Jesus saw the grief-stricken mother just behind the bier. This miracle came from his sympathy with human suffering. His eye affected his heart.

Luke often uses the words "the Lord" whereas the other Gospel writers do not refer to Jesus in this manner.

This woman may not even have known Jesus. This was a miracle of compassion.

There is no word of her faith mentioned anywhere in the episode.

The Lord allayed her grief before the miracle. Sometimes the words, "weep not" are used in a routine way, but this is not how Jesus used them. He spoke for her relief. He was not chiding her. His sympathy was not passive, but as we see shortly, very active. When Jesus said, "weep not," it was not merely a request. It was the beginning of an exercise of his power. For Christ that day displayed his *pity* and his *power*.

We have three accounts of Jesus raising a person from the dead. The young girl who was raised from the dead had the beseeching of her father, Jairus. The raising of Lazarus involved the beseeching of his sisters, Mary and Martha. But this miracle at Nain was done without the mother's even asking. In fact, we have no word at all that she spoke.

As Jesus touched the bier, the funeral procession stopped. They stood still without a request from him. How the crowd must have been amazed that he should touch the bier! Jewish rulers thought that such an act would bring corruption. But Jesus touched him just as he had touched the lepers whom no one else would go near.

Imagine what the disciples of Jesus must have thought! They had seen him heal the crippled, make the blind see, the deaf hear, the insane restored to reason. But could he bring back the dead?

Notice the brevity of Jesus' statement, "Young man, I say unto thee, Arise."

As soon as Christ said that, the dead youth sat up and spoke. There was no doubt that the young man had been dead. He had not just fainted. He was being carried out on his way to burial.

What the youth said we will never know. But perhaps he praised the Lord and spoke lovingly to his mother. Evidently the young man went back to his natural sphere of life. We know that Jesus delivered him to his mother, rather than keeping him in the company of his disciples. This fact shows that Jesus took instant care of him after raising him from the dead.

Now the mourning widow was turned into a thankful mother.

Those around became afraid, but above their fear was the compelling need to glorify God. They cried, "A great prophet has risen among us." Perhaps they were thinking of Elijah and Elisha.

Fear is often spoken of in the New Testament, but it is not a paralyzing fear—rather it is proper and creative.

The people acclaimed Jesus, and his fame spread the country over even into Judea. But his popularity brought only deeper hostility on the part of the Jewish rulers.

We can readily see that Christ was doing good every day. He never lost a day. We also learn from this miracle the great blessing that we can receive without even asking.

We also learn that, not only in this physical sense but also in a spiritual, that Christ has the power to raise us in the same manner when we are dead in sin.

Why was this silent woman included in the privileged group of twelve women with whom Jesus spoke—in a time when a rabbi speaking to a woman in public was unheard of?

Perhaps Jesus singled her out because she was so filled with sorrow. She had lost all of her loved ones. She seemed without hope. Not only was she bereaved of all family companionship, wrapped in loneliness, but now she had no one to help make her a living. She might be reduced to begging at the same gate she was now passing through with her dead son.

Jesus may also have spoken to her, thinking it necessary to do this, before he brought the young man back to life and delivered him to her.

Perhaps Jesus spoke to her *before* the miracle to teach that she must shut out grief, and think not of herself, in order to experience a miracle.

Although the woman thus blessed spoke no recorded words, we cannot correctly say that she had no faith. Jesus may have known that her heart was filled with faith.

Where is the current counterpart of this sorrowing woman? Perhaps she is among the largest group today of any of the twelve kinds of women with whom Jesus spoke.

For think of the countless instances where a woman, like this widow at Nain, stands at the open grave of her last family member. There are many women who are sole survivors. Many, many feminine hearts today know what it is to have lost a husband and later are giving up their only son.

So, let every modern woman take heart if she is left alone by death. Let her hear again the words of Jesus ringing down the centuries, gently pleading, "Weep not." For there will be a resurrection of their loved ones one fair day, too.

Also there may be grieving mothers who are single parents, who know that their sons are dead in sin. There are so many temptations for young men today—drugs, alcohol, sexual permissiveness.

But then come the consoling words, "Weep not."

They, too, in Christ can arise and be delivered to their mothers!

4

The Woman Who Anointed Jesus' Feet

The Woman Who Loved Much

Luke 7:36-50

And one of the Pharisees desired him that he would eat with him. And he went into the Pharisee's house, and sat down to meat.

And, behold, a woman in the city, which was a sinner, when she knew that Jesus sat at meat in the Pharisee's house, brought an alabaster box of ointment,

And stood at his feet behind him weeping, and began to wash his feet with tears, and did wipe them with the hairs of her head, and kissed his feet, and anointed them with the ointment.

Now when the Pharisee which had bidden him saw it, he spake within himself, saying, This man, if he were a prophet, would have known who and what manner of woman this is that toucheth him: for she is a sinner.

And Jesus answering said unto him, Simon, I have somewhat to say unto thee. And he saith, Master, say on.

There was a certain creditor which had two debtors: the one owed five hundred pence, and the other fifty.

And when they had nothing to pay, he frankly forgave them both. Tell me therefore, which of them will love him most?

Simon answered and said, I suppose that he, to whom he forgave most. And he said unto him, Thou hast rightly judged.

And he turned to the woman, and said unto Simon, Seest thou this woman? I entered into thine house, thou gavest me no water for my feet: but she hath washed my feet with tears, and wiped them with the hairs of her head.

Thou gavest me no kiss: but this woman since the time I came in hath not ceased to kiss my feet.

My head with oil thou didst not anoint: but this woman hath anointed my feet with ointment.

Wherefore I say unto thee, Her sins, which are many, are forgiven; for she loved much: but to whom little is forgiven, the same loveth little.

And he said unto her, Thy sins are forgiven.

And they that sat at meat with him began to say within themselves, Who is this that forgiveth sins also? And he said to the woman, Thy faith hath saved thee; go in peace.

Why did Jesus select this sinful woman as one of the chosen twelve with whom he would speak? (Some commentators feel that this unnamed woman was Mary of Bethany, the sister of Martha and Lazarus. See John 11:1-46.)

Perhaps the incident itself, if studied in depth, will reveal the answer.

One of the most touching and poignant scenes in the Gospels is that of this sinful woman coming in thankful love to anoint the feet of Jesus.

Every phase of this brief account paints an unforgettable vignette of devotion and penitence.

First of all, we note that Jesus had accepted the invitation of Simon the Pharisee to eat with him in his home. Christ always goes where he is invited. We should examine our own hearts and homes to discover if Christ is always a welcome guest there. On our better days, of course, we feel that we would love to have Christ sit down at our table with us.

It would be pleasing to have him in our family circle when there are fresh linens on the table, chicken ready and roasted properly, a cake that didn't fall waiting to be sliced, when all has gone well at work, and the children are not kicking each other under the table.

But would we leave the Master uninvited if the sink were stopped up, if we had missed a beauty appointment, if our elementary school picnicker had acquired a generous case of poison ivy?

Let's try, even as Simon did, desiring Christ to sit down with us, most especially when we eat. For a table can be an altar to the Lord.

Now, as the formal banquet proceeded at Simon's home, the woman of the story entered. Maybe she recognized some of the guests; they, too, might have known who she was because of her attire and her painted face.

Her approach showed that not only was she a caring person, but also a very courageous one.

For Jesus' ministry was at this time in what we call the second period of the Galilean ministry. This was a period when he was most popular. Throngs were always about him, pushing, scrambling, seeking to see him. She had to make her way to him through the crowd by force and drive.

This particular occasion must have involved a formal banquet, for it was at gatherings of this sort that the uninvited crowds came as spectators. The city in which this episode took place is unnamed, but it seems according to the Scriptures preceding, that it must have been Capernaum.

The first description we have of the woman is that she was a sinner. The accepted meaning of the word *sinner* as used here is prostitute.

What if we read no further and always called this woman, appearing so dramatically here, nothing more than a sinner?

So often we identify people by one term only. Someone's name is mentioned and one word may come to our minds—liar. Another person's name may be mentioned and we think of one word—stingy. We don't always hasten to add "liar—but generous in time of need"; stingy, but honest.

What one word would we have to live with if people identified us with only a single bad quality?

But fortunately we learn that this woman, a sinner, had so much love in her heart that there was no room for frugality. She came with an alabaster box of ointment. Alabaster was an expensive, white species of gypsum, not as hard as marble, probably found in Damascus. The ointment she used is usually described as oil of myrrh, much more delicate than the olive oil commonly offered as an act of courtesy to worn travelers. It was costly, but not too costly for her Lord.

Again we conclude that this was a formal gathering, for the Scriptures say that she stood at his feet behind him. It was only at formal events that diners stretched out on couches in this manner, after removing their sandals.

Another characteristic of this unusual woman is revealed as she wept. She wept unashamedly in remorse over her sins and her joy in being with the Lord.

She also showed the reverence that she held in her heart as she kissed the feet of Jesus and anointed them.

Now the Pharisee came to the forefront. He could have destroyed all the ground the woman had gained thus far, if Jesus had not intervened.

The Pharisee not only lived then, but lives all about us today. He failed to see the woman—he only saw her stereotype.

Are we guilty of this same attitude? Have we stopped looking at individuals and see only their kind? Do we see all young people as delinquent? Do we think all old people are crochety? Do we view all rich people as greedy? Do we think all politicians are crafty?

I recall one incident of this nature that occurred during World War II. I was with my husband who was with the military in a state far distant from our native home. When I offered to help with a church project there, one of the long-standing members, an early settler there, asked me, "Oh, aren't you one of those Navy wives?" Her tone and expression chilled me into inaction!

Jesus reacts individually with persons, not classes. He never sets up barriers between himself and another according to convention.

This particular Pharisee in the story began pondering why Jesus let such a woman touch Him. Perhaps Simon was displeased that Jesus didn't classify people as he did. He began to doubt that Jesus knew what she was because He violated the approved way of rejecting her.

Of course, the truth was that Jesus knew more, not less, about the woman than the Pharisee did. Isn't it wonderful that Jesus knows more, not less, about us than those who criticize us?

When Jesus began to speak in this drama so long ago, the tempo of the scene changed.

First of all, Jesus was going to set Simon straight.

Whenever I read, though a hundred times

over, where Jesus says, "Simon, I have somewhat to say unto thee," I always wonder if Jesus were talking with me, would he have somewhat to say unto me, too. The sinful woman thought Jesus had somewhat to say unto her also.

At least Simon had the grace to ask Jesus to continue. I trust that I can do this, too, instead of shutting my ears when I think Christ is reproving me.

A parable follows in which Jesus illustrated to Simon, by Simon's own admission, that he who is forgiven much, loves much, in contrast to one forgiven only a small debt. It's always interesting to see the women whom Jesus, in his long, harried journey, took time out to commend. This praise is made even more significant by the fact that the compliments paid to this penitent woman are addressed to Simon, her accuser.

Jesus recognized her homage in three ways. First, the host had given him no water with which to wash his feet, yet the woman had washed his feet with her tears. Second, the host had not greeted him with a kiss, yet the woman had not ceased to kiss his feet. Third, the host did not anoint his head with oil yet the woman had anointed his feet with ointment.

The woman standing and listening must have relaxed as she heard these words of approval spoken about her, though not directly to her.

But then she must have held her breath tightly, her lips quivering, as Jesus continued talking to Simon, "Her sins, which are many . . ." Even then she must have thought, *Would Jesus condemn me?* Scenes of her sinful nature probably flashed through her mind, causing her painful regret and bitter remorse. She must have cried out in her own heart, *Why? Why? Why did I live like that?*

Then she stopped this woeful recalling, for the words of Jesus came to her as soothing as the oil of myrrh that she had applied, "Her sins, which are many, are forgiven."

She listened further. Simon must have looked puzzled. Next Jesus explained her deliverance from sin. Why was she forgiven? "For she loved much."

Naturally, this strange utterance caused Simon and his friends to wonder about who this man was who could forgive sins.

It is wonderful that the woman did not leave with just an indirect statement of forgiveness. She might have gone all the rest of her life wondering if she were truly, personally forgiven.

But then Jesus turned to her—he was speaking directly to her.

"Thy faith hath saved thee; go in peace."

Why would he select this woman as one of the chosen few with whom he would speak directly?

Why a woman of the streets? Why a woman with many sins?

Surely, with so many, many feminine hearts desiring to speak with Jesus, this woman must have been very special to take up Jesus' time. She was special!

First of all, she came in the spirit of grateful love and sorrowful repentance. Second, she had rare courage to appear before a group teeming with self-righteousness. Third, she was generous. She presented a costly gift. Fourth, she was reverent in her regard for Jesus, humbly kissing his feet. Fifth, she had patience to listen to Jesus talking with Simon about her.

How well she was rewarded for these virtues, as the scene is concluded when Jesus speaks directly to her. "Thy faith hath saved thee; go in peace."

So with faith she went on her way rejoicing—a new life ahead! What a banquet that turned out to be!

Where is the counterpart of this unusual woman today? This woman had faith, love, repentance, courage, generosity, reverence, and patience. She was lifted from degradation to peace in a single night nearly two thousand years ago.

She lives in the heart of every woman who has missed the way, whose sins are many, whose life is all fouled up. For Jesus says to every modern woman with like compassion, "You, too, if you love much, can have your sins forgiven. You, too, if you have faith, can be saved. You, too, can go in peace."

Just for the offering, think of the gleaning.

What can we get for a bottle of ointment rightly given?

5

The Woman with an
Issue of Blood

THE SUFFERER

Matthew 9:20-22

And, behold, a woman, which was diseased with an issue of blood twelve years, came behind him, and touched the hem of his garment:

For she said within herself, If I may but touch his garment, I shall be whole.

But Jesus turned him about, and when he saw her, he said, Daughter, be of good comfort; thy faith hath made thee whole. And the woman was made whole from that hour.

Mark 5:25-34

And a certain woman, which had an issue of blood twelve years,

And had suffered many things of many physicians, and had spent all that she had, and was nothing bettered, but rather grew worse,

When she had heard of Jesus, came in the press behind, and touched his garment.

For she said, If I may touch but his clothes, I shall be whole.

And straightway the fountain of her blood was dried

up; and she felt in her body that she was healed of that plague.

And Jesus, immediately knowing in himself that virtue had gone out of him, turned him about in the press, and said, Who touched my clothes?

And his disciples said unto him, Thou seest the multitude thronging thee, and sayest thou, Who touched me?

And he looked round about to see her that had done this thing.

But the woman fearing and trembling, knowing what was done in her, came and fell down before him, and told him all the truth.

And he said unto her, Daughter, thy faith hath made thee whole; go in peace, and be whole of thy plague.

Luke 8:43-48

And a woman having an issue of blood twelve years, which had spent all her living upon physicians, neither could be healed of any,

Came behind him, and touched the border of his garment: and immediately her issue of blood stanched.

And Jesus said, Who touched me? When all denied, Peter and they that were with him said, Master, the multitude throng thee and press thee, and sayest thou, Who touched me?

And Jesus said, Somebody hath touched me: for I perceive that virtue is gone out of me.

And when the woman saw that she was not hid, she came trembling, and falling down before him, she declared unto him before all the people for what cause she had touched him, and how she was healed immediately.

And he said unto her, Daughter, be of good comfort: thy faith hath made thee whole; go in peace.

Think of all you have done in the last twelve years. You may recall marvelous trips you have made, promotions you have gained in your work, loved ones entering your family either by birth or by marriage, new homes or new places to live, maybe even a strengthened faith. You may have experienced a miracle or two during this period of more than a decade.

Now turn your thoughts to an unnamed woman who for twelve years had suffered with a dread disease, then called an issue of blood. She had spent all she had on physicians, but her condition had only worsened. Not only was she suffering bodily from this disease, but she was being destroyed emotionally. For this type of disease made her ceremonially unclean. She was out of society. She could not go to the Temple to offer sacrifices. If she touched anyone, that person would also be considered unclean. (See Lev. 15:25-27.)

Maybe all of her money was gone; she might have lost all of her friends when she lost her money. Her condition appeared painful, distressing, hopeless.

We see her as she came on the scene during the second period of Christ's Galilean ministry. She was filled with human despair, physical, mental, emotional, and spiritual.

Her story is wedged in between two parts of another miracle, the raising of the daughter of Jairus from the dead. Jesus had just returned from the country of the Gadarenes.

She probably had never seen Jesus. She may have heard of his miracles like the healing of Peter's mother-in-law, or the nobleman's son, or the slave of the Roman centurion.

But then she came to Jesus. How difficult it must have been for her to contact Jesus with all the throngs of people crowding about him. Many were curious about Jairus. They must have wondered what Jesus would do as this ruler of the synagogue walked along with Jesus in his rich robes.

We cannot refrain from wondering what this poor, sick woman was thinking as—tired, weary, and shy—she drew near to Jesus.

How could she muster this much faith to squeeze through the teeming crowds? Perhaps she was driven by her miserable suffering, the failure of human help, and the lack of money.

She must have thought in desperation, *I must touch Jesus.* This was her last outpost of help.

How brave she was, for most of the healings Jesus had performed had been for men. She knew the fearful power of prejudice for her sex and for her loathsome disease.

At this time Jesus had touched others in his healing miracles, but no one had yet touched him for a miracle to be performed. There was no precedent for this means of reaching Christ.

How we admire her determination! "If I may touch but his clothes, I shall be whole" (Mark 5:28). This was desperation pitted against faith. She permitted necessity to be above the law. She was cut off from man, but not from Christ. This bold procedure must have been nurtured by her confidence in Jesus.

She came from behind him and dared to touch the border of his garment! The Jews wore four tassels on their garments bordered in blue. (See Num. 15:38.) These four tassels were on the corners of the robe, one on each side, one on the front, and one on the back on the hem of the garment.

When she touched the garment, she was healed before a word was spoken! Before Jesus spoke she had already believed. She must have felt the instant healing when she touched his garment.

If the crowd noticed her in their scrambling, they must have been aghast at her unusual deed. Perhaps they waited to hear Jesus reprimand her.

They forgot that Jesus seems to count interruptions as blessings. His interest is always with the individual. He had stopped once to talk with Zacchaeus. He had paused at the roadside to heal blind Bartimaeus. Later on the cross, one individual drew his attention, the repentant thief hanging by him!

Notice the Lord's reaction to her touch. He knew all about her, yet he asked, "Who touched me?"

He must have wanted her great faith to be made public. This public declaration touches the heart more than a secretive healing would have.

In our mind's eye we can see this woman cringing, trying to escape into the crowd, when Jesus asked his awesome question.

The disciples were confounded by the Master's question. Peter was the spokesman who replied that they could not possibly tell in such a large crowd who had touched him. Others, filled with apprehension, denied that they were the bold ones who touched him. But then Jesus looked at her.

She learned that one can hide from mankind but not from Christ. Now the woman approached frightened and trembling. She fell down before Jesus and told him the truth, why she came, how she was healed immediately, and how she was free from disease.

So faith elicited touching and confessing, then commendation from Christ, for he said to her, "Daughter, be of good comfort; thy faith hath made thee whole. Go in peace, and be whole of thy plague."

As far as we can ascertain from the Scriptures, this is the only woman whom Jesus called "Daughter." So she must have been young. It would have been a shame if her faith had wavered, and she would have gone a lifetime in misery and suffering.

This woman's great faith must have affected Jairus, too. For just as Jesus was speaking to her, messengers came to say that Jairus' daughter had already died.

Had Jairus not just witnessed this miracle, he might have given up in despair of his daughter's being restored to life.

The beautiful words of Jesus, "Go in peace," are the same healing words that he spoke to the woman who anointed his feet.

Why did this woman of the privileged twelve get to speak with Jesus?

First of all, Jesus is never unmindful of suffering.

Secondly, she was filled with courage so strong that it took over from her fear and her distress.

Next, she dared to let her faith lead her into unconventional behavior. Too, her faith was true, believing faith. She knew that she was healed. Furthermore, she sensed the difference in man's withdrawal from her and Jesus' acceptance of her—just as she was. Last of all, she knew that touching Jesus not only meant belief, but it also meant confession.

Her worship involved declaring before the throng of people the truth of what she had done. No wonder that Jesus gave her three benedictions—comfort, wholeness, and peace!

Where does this woman live among the women of modern society?

We can see her most anywhere we choose to look.

Hospitals and doctors' offices are filled with women like this woman, battling diseases that have taken their toll on them for many years.

Some of these women also have diseases with a stigma barring them from friends and loved ones—social diseases, dread contagious diseases, mental breakdowns, emotional instability. These too are set apart in special hospitals or are confined in institutions.

These women of today have also gone from one physician to another and have perhaps have spent all they have.

Women of today, like this woman of Galilee, must practice humble faith. They must ignore the crowds who pass them by in their search to reach Jesus.

They too must not be afraid of touching and confessing.

Especially, if one's illness is related to sinful living, the women of today must realize that when Jesus looks at them, they must acknowledge what they have done.

If today's throng of women who are suffering will fall at the feet of Jesus, they too can know instant healing. They will feel the unspeakable joy of his words once again and experience comfort, wholeness, and peace.

6

The Daughter of Jairus

The Dearly Beloved

Matthew 9:18-19,23-26

While he spake these things unto them, behold, there came a certain ruler, and worshipped him, saying, My daughter is even now dead: but come and lay thy hand upon her, and she shall live. . . .

And Jesus arose, and followed him, and so did his disciples.

And when Jesus came into the ruler's house, and saw the minstrels and the people making a noise,

He said unto them, Give place: for the maid is not dead, but sleepeth. And they laughed him to scorn.

But when the people were put forth, he went in, and took her by the hand, and the maid arose.

And the fame hereof went abroad into all that land.

Mark 5:21-24,35-43

And when Jesus was passed over again by ship unto the other side, much people gathered unto him: and he was nigh unto the sea.

And, behold, there cometh one of the rulers of the synagogue, Jairus by name; and when he saw him, he fell at his feet,

And besought him greatly, saying, My little daughter lieth at the point of death: I pray thee, come and lay thy hands on her, that she may be healed; and she shall live.

And Jesus went with him; and much people followed him, and thronged him. . . .

While he yet spake, there came from the ruler of the synagogue's house certain which said, Thy daughter is dead: why troublest thou the Master any further?

As soon as Jesus heard the word that was spoken, he saith unto the ruler of the synagogue, Be not afraid, only believe.

And he suffered no man to follow him, save Peter, and James, and John the brother of James.

And he cometh to the house of the ruler of the synagogue, and seeth the tumult, and them that wept and wailed greatly.

And when he was come in, he saith unto them, Why make ye this ado, and weep? the damsel is not dead, but sleepeth.

And they laughed him to scorn. But when he had put them all out, he taketh the father and the mother of the damsel, and them that were with him, and entereth in where the damsel was lying.

And he took the damsel by the hand, and said unto her, Talitha cumi; which is, being interpreted, Damsel, I say unto thee, arise.

And straightway the damsel arose, and walked; for she was of the age of twelve years. And they were astonished with a great astonishment.

And he charged them straitly that no man should know it; and commanded that something should be given her to eat.

Luke 8:41-42,49-56

And, behold, there came a man named Jairus, and he was a ruler of the synagogue: and he fell down at

Jesus' feet, and besought him that he would come into his house:

For he had only one daughter, about twelve years of age, and she lay a dying. But as he went the people thronged him. . . .

While he yet spake, there cometh one from the ruler of the synagogue's house, saying to him, Thy daughter is dead; trouble not the Master.

But when Jesus heard it, he answered him, saying, Fear not: believe only, and she shall be made whole.

And when he came into the house, he suffered no man to go in, save Peter, and James, and John, and the father and the mother of the maiden.

And all wept, and bewailed her: but he said, Weep not; she is not dead, but sleepeth.

And they laughed him to scorn, knowing that she was dead.

And he put them all out, and took her by the hand, and called, saying, Maid, arise.

And her spirit came again, and she arose straightway: and he commanded to give her meat.

And her parents were astonished: but he charged them that they should tell no man what was done.

Perhaps the tenderest scene in which Jesus spoke to women is when he addressed this young girl, the daughter of Jairus. She is the youngest woman recorded as spoken directly to by Jesus.

Jesus and his disciples had returned to Capernaum from across the lake in the land of the Gadarenes. Throngs of people had gathered there welcoming Jesus back by the sea.

In the midst of this reunion there appeared

one of the rulers of the synagogue at Capernaum. This man, Jairus, came himself. He did not send a servant. Jairus may have been the person who supervised the conduct of worship in the synagogue. His name is derived from the name Jair, a chief of the lineage of Joseph. (See Num. 32:41.)

Jairus must have been knowledgeable in the teachings and miracles of Jesus. That's why he came to ask Jesus to heal his daughter.

He approached Jesus reverently, falling at his feet and worshiping him. Perhaps Jairus sensed that to receive mercy, one must give honor. He recognized Christ as a healer. He came pleading for his daughter who was dying.

Jairus certainly had faith in Jesus, or he would not have come to him beseeching. However, his faith apparently was not as great as that of the centurion whose servant Jesus had healed. Jairus felt that Jesus must go home with him in order to heal his young daughter. He was not quite up to believing in long-distance miracles.

Jesus left immediately with Jairus. Maybe the father's urgent plea had a special effect upon him. Mark has Jairus saying, "My little daughter." Later in the story Mark tells us that the young girl was twelve years old. Luke indicated that she was an only child. The father did not say, so we do not know what disease caused her to be so gravely ill.

Some may wonder why Jesus went with Jairus. Why did he think it was necessary to go home with this ruler before he could heal his daughter? He did not go home with the Syrophenician woman to heal her daughter. He did not go with the centurion to heal his servant. It seems that Jesus used a variety of methods in his healing miracles. He seemed to go along with the frame of mind and the temperament of those seeking him.

The disciples accompanied him. It was good for them to witness the miracles of Jesus to help them in their preaching.

But Jesus had no more than started walking along with Jairus and the crowds of people, when he was interrupted by the woman with the issue of blood.

We can imagine the consternation of Jairus, so anxious about his daughter, when Jesus was delayed by this ailing woman. The distraught father must have reasoned, *While he is stopping here, my daughter could be dying. He could heal this woman tomorrow or some other day.*

But Jairus, like all of us, had to learn patience in waiting for the miracles of Jesus.

If Jairus entertained such fears, as we imagine he did, he must have realized that his concern in the delay was not groundless.

For while Jesus was yet talking to this woman, who had touched the hem of his garment, there came people from the house of

Jairus to bring the sad news, "Thy daughter is dead: why troublest thou the Master any further?"

It is perhaps good that we do not have a glimpse of Jairus as these words were spoken. He must have been utterly dejected.

But before Jairus could speak, Jesus stepped in with his ever-encouraging words: "Be not afraid, ony believe."

Christ did not give the father time to doubt as hope was supplied. So Jairus must have straightened up again, stengthened by a renewed faith.

When the travelers reached the home of Jairus, the mourners were there. The musicians must have been playing their doleful tunes. Christ rebuked all the hurry, the confusion, and the noise.

In all the tumult Jesus said, "Why make ye this ado, and weep? the damsel is not dead, but sleepeth."

In response to this assurance, the mourners and wailers were not only skeptical, but they mocked Jesus. They laughed him to scorn. Those that were so ready to weep, now were ready to laugh.

Christ will not show his power to scoffers. So he expelled all of the bystanders except the parents of the girl and his "inner circle" of disciples—Peter, James, and John. These three disciples were permitted to go several places with Jesus where the other nine followers were not allowed to go. These three were on the mount of transfiguration with Jesus and were also in the garden of Gethsemane with the Lord.

These select few were escorted to the room where the young girl lay. So it was as witnesses of faith, not curiosity, that they would behold the miracle Jesus was about to perform.

Jesus took the young girl by the hand. Again we see Jesus unafraid to break the tradition of abhorrence of the dead. In the miracles of Jesus he took the one in need by the hand. Jesus knew the power of touch long before the modern psychologists learned of the magic of this communication.

As he held her hand, Jesus spoke Aramaic words to her, "Talitha cumi." This phrase means, "Damsel, I say unto thee, arise."

As soon as Jesus touched the girl and spoke, immediately she arose and walked. Then Jesus acting through kindness, commanded them to give her meat to eat.

Again we notice that Jesus is concerned with our physical necessities, as well as our spiritual needs.

The parents were astonished at this tremendous miracle.

Jesus charged that no person should hear of this, but this happening spread abroad anyway. Jesus likely asked that this miracle be kept secret to protect the young girl. He wanted to spare her all of the questions, the people invading her privacy, and the curious onlookers, who would leave her no moment to herself.

Thus, Jesus set his seal on human affection, pity for a breaking heart.

Jesus also in this miracle reveals that parental affection may stimulate and strengthen faith and piety. Jesus is the best refuge for the hearts of troubled parents. This young girl must have been agreeable, helpful, and loved, for the neighbors wept and wailed her so greatly.

Now, why was this young girl, the youngest of all the twelve females with whom Jesus spoke, so special to Jesus?

Jesus may have chosen her to speak to because she was so young and innocent. Jesus may have wanted older women to realize that the young ones have an equal place in his heart, that there is no age group superior to any other in his eyes.

He seems here to have placed his seal on the power of youth, if youth will only arise.

Perhaps he spoke to this young girl because she must have been especially loving, dear, and sweet. Why else would her father, the dignified ruler of the synagogue, have humbled himself before Christ to plead for her?

We are not sure, but it could be that the young girl herself had so much faith that she implored her father to seek Jesus out for her healing. Maybe this is why Jairus wanted Jesus to go home with him, to see his daughter's faith.

How does this young woman, the youngest of all, find a place among the women of today? In the twentieth century, more than ever before, we see this woman everywhere among our youth.

She might be indicative of any young woman today who is dead in spirit. So many young girls, especially among affluent parents, have already experienced so many thrills that should have waited for a later time in their lives. This superimposing of adult life-styles on childhood leaves young girls lethargic, sophisticated, bored by the time they are twelve years old. They are dead in spirit. They have no goals, no purpose. Life seem trite to them. They are definitely in a youth slump, in a rut.

To all young girls who are languishing in a world that is no longer exciting to them in faith, purpose, and service, open your hearts to Jesus and hear again the words of endearment; "Talitha cumi." "Damsel, I say unto thee, arise."

Then the miracle will happen all over again for you. In the buoyancy of youth, Christ-centered as it should be, you will arise and walk to glory with God!

7

The Syrophenician Woman

A Woman Driven

Matthew 15:21-28

Then Jesus went thence, and departed into the coasts of Tyre and Sidon.

And, behold a woman of Canaan came out of the same coasts, and cried unto him, saying, Have mercy on me, O Lord, thou son of David; my daughter is grievously vexed with a devil.

But he answered her not a word. And his disciples came and besought him saying, Send her away; for she crieth after us.

But he answered and said, I am not sent but unto the lost sheep of the house of Israel.

Then came she and worshipped him, saying, Lord, help me.

But he answered and said, It is not meet to take the children's bread, and to cast it to dogs.

And she said, Truth, Lord: yet the dogs eat of the crumbs which fall from their masters' table.

Then Jesus answered and said unto her, O woman, great is thy faith: be it unto thee even as thou wilt. And her daughter was made whole from that very hour.

Mark 7:24-30

And from thence he arose, and went into the borders

of Tyre and Sidon, and entered into an house, and would have no man know it: but he could not be hid.

For a certain woman, whose young daughter had an unclean spirit, heard of him, and came and fell at his feet:

The woman was a Greek, a Syrophenician by nation; and she besought him that he would cast forth the devil out of her daughter.

But Jesus said unto her, let the children first be filled: for it is not meet to take the children's bread and to cast it unto the dogs.

And she answered and said unto him, Yes, Lord: yet the dogs under the table eat of the children's crumbs.

And he said unto her, For this saying go thy way; the devil is gone out of thy daughter.

And when she was come to her house, she found the devil gone out, and her daughter laid upon the bed.

In one of the sweetest stories in the Gospels there appears the Syrophenician woman, a woman driven.

This story could well be called the six Cs. For it involves a study of clans, creeds, clarification, conquering of rejection, cleverness, and compensation.

Before the woman came to Jesus, he was seeking respite on the borders of Tyre and Sidon. He didn't even want anyone to know that he was in a particular house. But he could not be hidden. This is the only record we have of Jesus' being this far away from the main centers of his ministry. This was in his year of opposition.

Now entered the woman of Canaan, a Greek, a Syrophenician. These are all her rightful titles. She was a descendant of the people of Canaan whom Joshua had dispossessed. She was called Greek which means Gentile. She was Syrophenician for Phenicia was then a part of Syria. These people were called Phenicians of Syria to distinguish them from Phenicians of Libya. The chief Phenician cities were Tyre and Sidon.

When she cried out to Jesus, "O Lord, thou son of David," she acknowledges him as the Messiah. Yet the Phenicians worshiped Ashtoroth, as the giver of life, which deity permitted them to do almost any evil. This woman may have been the first heathen blessed by the Lord face-to-face.

Why did this woman of another race seek out Christ?

She was driven—driven by misery, by family distress. She seems to have been a widow since she did not mention her husband.

She sought mercy first for herself and then for her daughter. She was not ashamed to relate her misery as she said that her daughter was vexed with a devil, an unclean spirit. She came for healing. A need for her daughter drove her to Christ.

Immediately we discern the discouragement she faced, maybe more so than in any other scene during the ministry of Jesus.

Prior to this we read of his compassion and

his feeding of the five thousand. So there was a shock when first of all Jesus did not answer her a word.

But his apparent indifference made her prayer even more urgent. She drew nearer to him, falling at his feet, and beseeching him, "Lord, help me!" She did not blame Christ here. She blamed herself. She did not argue with Christ that she was not of the chosen group, the house of Israel. Instead of argument, she used prayer as her defense.

The fervor of her prayer lay in its brevity: "Help me!" If this Scripture were being read for the first time, we could not refrain from thinking that, after this last earnest plea, there would be some assurance from Jesus.

Yet his next words to her seem to us a further reproach, a cutting off of all hope, "It is not meet to take the children's bread, and to cast it to dogs."

It seems that she might have despaired at this statement when Jesus in apparent contempt referred to her people as "dogs."

But notice how she handled this last discouragement. Only her faith and her humility helped her bear this final restriction. It seems that she took everything bad that was said and put the best construction on it. What was said against her, she made count for her.

She simply acknowledged that what Jesus said was true.

She must have wondered, *Is Jesus after all*

like our Canaanite gods? Is Jesus trying my faith? We begin to think of Abraham and his trial of faith.

What if this woman, rebuked by the silence of Jesus, had run away in anger? Next the disciples added to her distress. They must certainly have considered their own comfort rather than the plea of the poor woman. Yet, think of the miracles that they had already seen Jesus perform—the blind seeing, the dumb speaking, the healing of the woman with the issue of blood, even the raising from the dead of the daughter of Jairus.

But because she was annoying them with her cries, they said, "Send her away."

Still she did not leave. She stayed in spite of the taunts.

As Jesus began to speak, she must have thought, *Surely he will rebuke his disciples. He will answer my plea for mercy for me and my daughter.* But not so—his response was strange.

He seemed to be speaking partly to the disciples and partly to her. He explained that he was sent to the lost sheep of the house of Israel.

Why did he withhold his mercy? He seemed almost to be arguing against her since she was not Jewish—not of the house of Israel by race.

Yet in all humility she expressed gratitude for even the crumbs that fell from the table. She was on the threshold of learning that the greatest mercies come to us when we consider ourselves as the least—like Gideon who said, "I am the least in my father's house" (Judg. 6:15). He then became one of the greatest judges.

Her faith made her expect at least the crumbs. Her humility was the ground on which blessings would pour out.

Only after this complete abandonment of pride when she answered, "Truth, Lord: yet the dogs under the table eat of the children's crumbs," did Jesus turn her despair into joy, as he then commended her faith.

This woman was wise, humble, patient, and courageous. But Jesus commended only her faith. "O woman, great is thy faith." These other admirable attributes grew out of her deep faith.

Her reward was twofold. Jesus commended her faith and cured her daughter.

Few have heard him say, "Be it unto thee even as thou wilt."

When Jesus told her to go her way and that the devil was gone out of her daughter, she went in confidence. When she reached home, the devil had gone out of her daughter, and the girl was resting and quiet in bed. This was a remote-control miracle. Christ can conquer Satan at a distance. The young girl may have been healed even as Jesus began to talk with the mother and saw her remarkable faith. Any way, this woman had been a conductor from Christ to the daughter.

There can be no doubt why this dear woman was one of the chosen twelve with whom Jesus spoke. She was so full of faith, courage, openness, humility, patience, reverence, peacefulness, that he could not pass her by.

Where do we find the counterpart of this woman in the rush of today's society?

She may be the most prevalent type of all the kinds of women with whom Jesus spoke. She could be you or I, our next-door neighbor, the PTA president, the woman checking our groceries at the supermarket, the operator helping us with long-distance calls, any woman anywhere who has faith enough to intercede for those she loves who are in trouble.

Another counterpart of this Syrophenician woman could be some woman from a minority group who feels that she too has to eat the crumbs from under the table. Maybe she does not have the best housing conditions, good medical treatment, or superb schools for her children.

Here is the woman who has the courage to ask the Lord for mercy for her child. So many women all over the world are praying for their children who have gone astray.

Like this woman, we must remember that all prayers are not answered instantly. We may need to keep on praying and advance closer to

Jesus as this woman did in reverent worship. The youths we pray for may not immediately change their life-styles or give up harmful patterns,. We must become more fervent in our prayers, acknowledging our own weaknesses.

There are many women today who like this woman must suffer an apparent period of silence as prayers seem to go unanswered. If faith prevails, time will usher in benefits from prayer for others in untold numbers.

Today the Lord has mercy reserved for faithful mothers just as he did on the borders of Tyre and Sidon.

Troubled mothers of children under the power of sin can be assured that their faith is not rejected. If need drives us to Christ, he will not drive us away. It is good for us to carry the troubles of others to him. If the Lord grants mercy to our children, he will grant mercy to us, the parents, too.

There are women who must also bear the further disapproval of those around them as they seek help for their children through prayer. There will be those who ridicule them. There will be those who tire of hearing about their pleas.

It may seem at times that the ear of the Lord is turned to those who already have the best in life—like this woman must have thought about the house of Israel. But if intercessory prayer continues, and humility abounds, the Lord will not turn away from the plea, "Help me!"

Perhaps there are women who may have to say, "Give us the crumbs."

When the full acknowledgment of one's humility comes, women of today will also hear the Lord say, "Great is thy faith."

The devil will also go out of the daughters and sons also. Maybe marriages will be saved, drugs discarded, bottles thrown away.

Women of today, we are in the most blessed category of women to whom Jesus spoke. We can hear the words of the Savior echoing down the centuries to us, "O woman, how great is thy faith: be it unto thee even as thou wilt."

8

The Woman Taken in Adultery

A Woman Spared

John 8:1-11

Jesus went unto the mount of Olives.

And early in the morning he came again unto the temple, and all the people came unto him; and he sat down, and taught them.

And the scribes and Pharisees brought unto him a woman taken in adultery; and when they had set her in the midst,

They say unto him, Master, this woman was taken in adultery, in the very act.

Now Moses in the law commanded us, that such should be stoned; but what sayest thou?

This they said, tempting him, that they might have to accuse him. But Jesus stooped down, and with his finger wrote on the ground, as though he heard them not.

So when they continued asking him, he lifted up himself, and said unto them, He that is without sin among you, let him first cast a stone at her.

And again he stooped down, and wrote on the ground.

And they which heard it, being convicted by their own conscience, went out one by one, beginning at the eldest, even unto the last: and Jesus was left alone, and the woman standing in the midst.

When Jesus had lifted up himself, and saw none but the woman, he said unto her, Woman, where are those thine accusers? hath no man condemned thee?

She said, No man, Lord. And Jesus said unto her, Neither do I condemn thee: go, and sin no more.

This encounter surely must have occurred in the last part of the Galilean ministry of Jesus.

Jesus had come from the Mount of Olives early in the morning to teach in the Temple.

As he sat there teaching, throngs of people came to hear him. Then this dramatic scene unfolded.

The scribes and Pharisees broke in on Jesus' discourse as the people were listening to his doctrine.

They brought in a woman caught in adultery and cast her into the crowd before Jesus. The details of this rude interruption are omitted in the Scriptures. But several strong men probably came dragging along one frail woman, maybe by the hair of the head, twisting her arms, pushing her roughly through the crowd to Jesus. She may have been scuffling, tearful, trying to hide her face from the crowd.

Why did these stern upholders of the law bring this woman to Jesus? It seems they were not so interested in upholding morality. This could not have been their chief concern, for her partner in adultery was also guilty, but no mention is made of him. He was, according to Mosaic law, to suffer the same penalty that would be given to the woman. (See Lev. 20:10 and Deut. 22:21.) The penalty for adultery was stoning.

Once they had thrown her into the crowd to face Jesus, they lost no time in exclaiming their purpose.

They began by letting him know that they wanted him to judge this woman for her act because they called him, "Master." Near this time they called him "deceiver" (Matt. 27:63).

Jesus has insight into hearts and motives. He knew their purpose. If they had no ulterior motive, it would have been unnecessary for them to come at all. For they stated that she was taken in the very act of adultery. They did not need Jesus to judge her. If they could prove that she was in the act of adultery, the punishment would be sure and swift. They had witnesses right there. They did not need Jesus to convict her. The law was clear.

Naturally we assume that they were there to test Jesus.

They were confronting him with someone who had broken the law of Moses. So, what would the answer of Jesus be? Would he uphold the law or the sinner?

Since the scribes and Pharisees knew that she was a sinner, she was the right one for them to bring before Jesus, to test Jesus.

This incident was in some ways the most vicious of all the trials Jesus had to face.

For if Jesus had agreed that the poor woman who committed adultery should be put to death, he would have been breaking the Roman law. The Romans had denied the Jews the right to administer capital punishment.

On the other hand, if Jesus had agreed that the sinful woman should be put to death, he would be contradicting what he had been preaching concerning mercy and compassion to publicans and sinners.

They reasoned further that if Jesus did not condemn the guilty woman, or if he asked that she be spared the death penalty, he would then be denying the Mosaic law. He would no longer be among friends, for these people in the crowd were loyal Jews, strictly adhering to the Mosaic law.

Furthermore, Jesus would again be contradicting his teachings, for he had said that he had not come to destroy the law, but to fulfill it.

But Jesus was not caught in this trap laid so skillfully by the scribes and Pharisees. He was well aware that they used the law of Moses to hide their own spiritual laxity.

If we had not read this Scripture before, we would be fearful here. It seemed that Jesus had no alternative. We would think that this was a step nearer the cross.

The intruders put the question bluntly to Jesus, "This woman was taken in adultery, in the very act. Now Moses in the law commanded us, that such should be stoned: but what sayest thou?"

Imagine the distraught woman waiting for words from Jesus. She must have been trembling, thinking in revulsion of the horror of being stoned, rocks squashing her skin, her body becoming a bloody pulp, and, finally, being ground into the earth, with the men mocking her as they killed her.

Imagine the scribes and Pharisees waiting, smirking, also for the words of Jesus. They must have thought how at last they had caught him without an avenue of escape. Now either the Roman government would apprehend him or the mob would turn against him, maybe even stoning him.

Imagine the people in the crowd also waiting for the words of Jesus. They must have been torn between pity for the woman, fear of the evil scribes and Pharisees, and the longing for Jesus to give the right answer.

All of these three kinds of participants in this drama must have held their breath as they waited for Jesus to answer. A life or lives, a way of life, a philosophy—all hung in the balance, depending on his answer. Many would not be the same after he spoke.

But Jesus answered not a word. The silence must have been all but unbearable!

Why was Jesus silent?

Did he want to shift the interest from the poor woman to himself?

Jesus then stooped down and wrote on the

ground as though he had not even heard the demanding question. This was the only time we have any record of his writing anywhere. This is a good lesson for us not to be so quick to speak. The scribes and Pharisees were not so easily put aside. They keep on asking Jesus, hounding him.

Then Jesus revealed his true wisdom. He neither condemned nor condoned the guilty woman. He faced the accusers with this soul-searing statement, "He that is without sin among you, let him first cast a stone at her."

For Jesus was well-versed in the Jewish law. The accusers evidently had proof that the woman was guilty of adultery. Her act took place during the Feast of the Tabernacles. At this festive time people were staying in the booths; there was much jollity and carousing about. It was a time that would induce adultery among those of loose living.

But this is what Jesus must have had in mind (Deut. 17:7). In the Jewish court, the witnesses had to be of good character or their testimony did not stand up. If the witnesses were found to be of unsavory character, the penalty against them was heavy.

Now Jesus stooped down and wrote again on the ground. At that time the attention must have gone from him to the crowd.

What did Jesus write in the dust there on this tense day? Did he write of the guilt of the accusers one by one? Could they have been guilty of adultery also? Or robbery? Or violence?

What he wrote no one knows, but we do know that one by one the accusers left the crowd until only Jesus and the woman remained.

They had set out to accuse Jesus, but it turned out that they accused themselves. They remind us of the fact that those who are indulgent in sin are always quick to persecute others.

The eldest of the scribes and the Pharisees left first. We are not sure if this were the custom for the eldest to leave first, or whether being older he was the first to have his conscience bother him. The conscience is God's guard of the soul. Jesus had succeeded in showing them to themselves. They didn't like the picture they saw.

We further view what happened to the scribes and Pharisees, as they stole away from the presence of Jesus and the woman.

We don't know what happened to the people thronging about. Maybe they left rejoicing that the woman was allowed to live. They may have been glad to see the scribes and Pharisees humiliated. But surely, most of all, they must have been grateful that Jesus was not only kind but that he was also exceedingly wise.

When Jesus raised up, he saw no one except the accused woman. He invited her to speak.

He addressed her, "Woman, where are those

thine accusers? hath no man condemned thee?

Her reaction is interesting. She called him Lord. She did not try to escape. She could have run to safety among the throngs of people. She also did not attack her accusers. She merely replied to the Lord that no man had condemned her.

She still must have been fearful that Jesus would condemn her or at least lecture her. Her gross sin had been brought to light. She could not testify: "Not guilty."

But Jesus' answer to her was tender:

Neither do I condemn thee: go, and sin no more."

It could be that Jesus looked into her heart and knew that she might have slipped into this misdeed. He knew she was sorry it had happened and would not let it happen again. Jesus did not rank sin in the same order as the scribes and Pharisees. In blotting out her sin, Jesus trusted her to do better. Jesus set her free from condemnation but called her to do right.

He dismissed her with caution.

We can see her that night going to bed with a great peace in her heart and resolve in her spirit to sin no more.

Why was this sinful woman one of the blessed women with whom Jesus spoke in his earthly ministry?

Maybe the conditions under which she committed this sin aroused the pity of Jesus for

her. We are not familiar with her background
or the forces that may have pressured her. But
Jesus knew and there was only compassion,
instead of disgust, towards her because of the
circumstances.

Maybe Jesus wished to talk with her because the men had treated her so roughly.
Maybe Jesus wanted to show the throngs of
people the difference in the attitude of the
angry men and the understanding that he had
for her.

Perhaps he talked with her because she was
not vindictive. She did not accuse those who
had treated her so shabbily.

She also had courage because she stayed
with Jesus, even though she did not know
what he might say to her. She did not run
away!

Where is this type of woman among us today? What is the message of Jesus to similar
women now?

This message of understanding and caution
comes across as clearly to us as it did to this
trembling woman on the Temple grounds so
long ago.

To all women who have committed adultery,
whatever the circumstances: if they are penitent and wish to start a new life-style, especially if they have been abused by coarse men
and if they acknowledge the Lord, come the
words of Jesus all over again, "Neither do I
condemn thee: go, and sin no more."

What a solace that phrase must be to those on the back streets, in the flurry of youthful temptations, those led on by alcohol or drugs to a sordid way of life.

"Go thou and sin no more" can raise the degraded to self-respect through Christ Jesus!

9

Martha

The Cumbered One

Luke 10:38-42

Now it came to pass, as they went, that he entered into a certain village: and a certain woman named Martha received him into her house.

And she had a sister called Mary, which also sat at Jesus' feet, and heard his word.

But Martha was cumbered about much serving, and came to him, and said, Lord, dost thou not care that my sister hath left me to serve alone? bid her therefore that she help me.

And Jesus answered and said unto her, Martha, Martha, thou art careful and troubled about many things:

But one thing is needful: and Mary hath chosen that good part, which shall not be taken away from her.

During his Perean ministry, Jesus entered a certain village which we presume was Bethany, since Martha was the hostess. This exquisite story is found only in the Gospel of Luke.

Jesus often visited Bethany which was only about two and one-half miles from Jerusalem.

This quiet hamlet must have seemed like a welcome refuge to him. There he could escape the noise, confusion, and worriment of larger cities.

Martha welcomed him into her home. The name Martha means "lady." Martha was the sister of Mary and Lazarus. This family must have loved Jesus dearly and always made him comfortable in their home. Martha appears to have been a widow. Some claim that she was the wife of Simon the leper. Martha apparently was older than Mary.

This is the intriguing story of two sisters who were very different in temperament and talent, though they both had a strong love for Jesus. They enacted this love in two separate ways.

Mary, we are told in the Scriptures, sat at Jesus' feet and listened to him teach. Mary longed for spiritual understanding. Mary wanted to receive the message from Jesus. Mary was somewhat like the disciple, John, whom Jesus loved in a special way. Mary enjoyed Christ; she had rest with him.

Martha, we must acknowledge, had many superb qualities. She, like Mary, wanted to please the Lord. But let us look at some of her characteristics which impelled her to be cross with the Lord, almost fussing at him.

Martha was industrious. She must have worked hard in the home in order to have guests. She had a practical nature. She let herself be distracted from Jesus by her many tasks. She must have wanted everything festive—special dishes, linens just so—for the visit of Jesus. No wonder she needed help for these tasks.

We would have to say that Martha seemed unquiet, always busy, the kind of person who would get up in the middle of a conversation to straighten a picture on the wall. Martha was most interested in producing food, beautiful decor, a clean house, and the like. Martha was restless, impatient, somewhat like the disciple Peter. We never think of Martha as being calm. In all her anxiety over having everything in order, she seemed to forget to enjoy Christ.

She was too concerned about worldly cares, and this is the preoccupation that causes much disturbance among families of any age. Martha was oversolicitous. Many of the details which troubled her were needless.

We see Martha at her lowest ebb when she reproved the Lord for not caring that Mary was not helping her. She commanded him to make Mary help her. We have to censure Martha here, for she was trying to pull the Lord onto her side and against Mary.

She was dreadfully wrong in wanting Mary to be just like her. Martha thought that she had the only right way to serve the Lord.

Martha wanted Jesus to blame Mary, but instead he blamed Martha. She seemed to want Jesus' approval for being angry with Mary.

Jesus' answer to Martha's demand was a reproach, but he softened it by calling her name, "Martha, Martha."

He blamed her for "much serving." It seems that Martha had done far more than was necessary, and nobody seemed to care about that except Martha herself. The Lord wanted Martha to concentrate on one thing that was important rather than wearing herself out on so many things.

Jesus told Martha there was just one needful thing. He must have meant receptive faith, for that was Mary's attitude when Jesus commended her choice. Jesus was concerned that Martha would bypass this best part in all of her hurry and bustle.

The story concludes without giving us the reaction of Martha to these soul-searching words of Jesus. However, for the strength we find exhibited by Martha later in the Scriptures, she must have heeded Jesus' advice.

Why was this anxious, preoccupied, fretful woman one of the women Jesus chose to speak with during his ministry?

It surely must have been that he looked beneath her bossiness, her flurry, her nervousness, to see the heart of a woman who wanted to serve, who wanted everything pretty, who longed to do extra things to please, who did not mind working hard. He must have wanted to put a few finishing touches on a gracious lady who needed to discard a few disagreeable habits.

Who are the modern Marthas? They are in innumerable homes of today. They run smooth homes, look after their children, carry food to the sick, feed the preachers, run the church kitchens, preside over the women's societies in missionary circles, organize PTA, take up collections for civic drives, serve on city beautification committees, and many other worthwhile tasks.

But the message is the same to modern women as it was to Martha—"What you are doing is good, but don't lose your soul in activity. Don't work so hard for the community that you are cross with your husband and your children. Remember that service to others goes along with talking to the Lord."

The One Whose Faith Was Enlightened

John 11:1-46

Now a certain man was sick, named Lazarus, of Bethany, the town of Mary and her sister Martha.

(It was that Mary which anointed the Lord with ointment, and wiped his feet with her hair, whose brother Lazarus was sick.)

Therefore his sisters sent unto him, saying, Lord, behold, he whom thou lovest is sick.

When Jesus heard that, he said, This sickness is not unto death, but for the glory of God, that the Son of God might be glorified thereby.

Now Jesus loved Martha, and her sister, and Lazarus.

When he had heard therefore that he was sick, he abode two days still in the same place where he was.

. . . .

Then when Jesus came, he found that he had lain in the grave four days already.

Now Bethany was nigh unto Jerusalem, about fifteen furlongs off:

And many of the Jews came to Martha and Mary, to comfort them concerning their brother.

Then Martha as soon as she heard that Jesus was coming, went and met him: but Mary sat still in the house.

Then said Martha unto Jesus, Lord, if thou hadst been here, my brother had not died.

But I know, that even now, whatsoever thou wilt ask of God, God will give it thee.

Jesus saith unto her, Thy brother shall rise again.

Martha saith unto him, I know that he shall rise again in the resurrection at the last day.

Jesus said unto her, I am the resurrection, and the life: he that believeth on me, though he were dead, yet shall he live.

And whosoever liveth and believeth in me shall never die. Believest thou this?

She saith unto him, Yea, Lord: I believe that thou art the Christ, the Son of God, which should come into the world.

And when she had so said, she went her way, and called Mary her sister secretly, saying, The Master is come, and calleth for thee.

As soon as she heard that, she arose quickly, and came unto him.

Now Jesus was not yet come into the town, but was in that place where Martha met him.

The Jews then which were with her in the house, and comforted her, when they saw Mary, that she rose up hastily and went out, followed her, saying, She goeth unto the grave to weep there.

Then when Mary was come where Jesus was, and saw him, she fell down at his feet, saying unto him, Lord, it thou hadst been here, my brother had not died.

When Jesus therefore saw her weeping, and the Jews also weeping which came with her, he groaned in the spirit, and was troubled,

And said, Where have ye laid him? They said unto him, Lord, come and see.

Jesus wept.

Then said the Jews, Behold how he loved him!

And some of them said, Could not this man, which opened the eyes of the blind, have caused that this man even should not have died?

Jesus therefore again groaning in himself cometh to the grave. It was a cave, and a stone lay upon it.

Jesus said, Take ye away the stone. Martha, the sister of him that was dead, saith unto him, Lord, by this time he stinketh: for he hath been dead four days.

Jesus saith unto her, Said I not unto thee, that, if thou wouldest believe, thou shouldest see the glory of God?

Then they took away the stone from the place where the dead was laid. And Jesus lifted up his eyes, and said, Father, I thank thee that thou hast heard me.

And I knew that thou hearest me always: but because of the people which stand by I said it, that they may believe that thou hast sent me.

And when he thus had spoken, he cried with a loud voice, Lazarus, come forth.

And he that was dead came forth, bound hand and foot with graveclothes: and his face was bound about with a napkin. Jesus saith unto them, Loose him, and let him go.

Then many of the Jews which came to Mary, and had seen the things which Jesus did, believed on him.

But some of them went their ways to the Pharisees, and told them what things Jesus had done.

This scene also occurred during the Perean ministry of Jesus. John is the only Gospel writer who relates this miracle. John describes seven miracles before the crucifixion. This is the last and the greatest of these.

In this story we will recognize that Martha has become stronger in faith.

Lazarus (whose name is a short form of Eleazar), the brother of Martha and Mary, was ill. The sisters sent for Jesus, but he delayed two days before he came. When he arrived at Bethany, he found that Lazarus had died and been buried four days.

Many people had visited the home to comfort Martha and Mary.

When Martha heard that Jesus was coming, she probably ran out to meet him, but Mary stayed in the house.

Again we view the same characteristics displayed in the sisters that Luke told us about. Martha was active and busy; she always had to be doing something. She had to go meet Jesus. She could not sit and wait.

On the other hand, Martha's arising and going to Jesus as she did indicates her new strength. Mary appeared a little selfish here as she sat and apparently thought of her grief.

Martha's first words to Jesus here could be taken in one of two ways. She might still have been the complainer, full of resentment, chiding Jesus for not being there on time. But perhaps we should give her the benefit of the doubt. She may have had greater faith when she said, "Lord, if thou hadst been here, my brother had not died."

When Jesus told her that her brother would rise again, she immediately thought of heaven.

But Jesus gave her further instruction, "I am the resurrection, and the life: he that believeth in me, though he were dead, yet shall he live."

Martha yielded then to what Jesus said, for she replied, "I believe that thou art the Christ, the Son of God."

After this Martha went back to tell Mary that Jesus was there. When Mary left to join Jesus, a large following of the mourners went with her.

When Mary reached Jesus, she voiced the exact words that Martha had spoken to him. However, Mary appeared more reverent as she fell at his feet and worshiped Jesus.

When Jesus saw Mary and the Jews with her weeping, he asked, "Where have ye laid him?"

We consider this question not directly to
Mary, but to the entire group, since the Scriptures read, "They said unto him, Lord, come
and see."

Jesus asked Mary no questions, as he did
Martha. For he asked Martha pointedly, "Believest thou this?"

But Mary's grief moved him. For we now ar-
rive at the shortest verse in the Bible.

"Jesus wept" (John 11:35).

So Martha got teaching from Jesus and Mary
got sympathy from him. It appears here that
Martha had precedence over Mary, since Jesus
spoke directly to the former.

But Mary had the consolation that, though
Jesus did not speak directly to her here, he
wept with her!

When Jesus came to Lazarus's grave in the
cave, he instructed, "Take ye away the stone."

Again Martha reverted to her old complain-
ing, missing the finest things. She, in the face
of what she must have thought would be a miracle, cautions, "Lord, by this time he stinks."

Again the Lord must reprove Martha. He
asked, "Said I not unto thee, that if thou
wouldest believe, thou shouldest see the glory
of God?"

Then Jesus prayed a prayer of gratitude to
the heavenly Father that the people standing
by might believe.

Then he commanded that Lazarus come
forth and directed further, "Loose him, and let

him go." Many who saw this believed, but some went to the Pharisees.

Martha has the distinction, except for Mary, the mother of Jesus, of being the only other "chosen woman" whom Jesus talked with on more than one occasion.

We presume that on the former occasion Jesus spoke with Martha to help her overcome some of her faith-sapping habit.

Why then did Jesus speak to Martha again at the raising of Lazarus from the dead?

It could have been necessary for Jesus to complete the loving advice he had given her when he earlier visited in her home.

She seemed to have had more faith than before, but Jesus was still concerned about her. He wanted to be sure of Martha as he asked her the searching question, "Believest thou this?"

Also, when Martha seemed to be thinking of the stench of the grave rather than the approaching miracle, Jesus had to remind her, "Didn't I say if you would believe, you would see the glory of God?"

Maybe Jesus couldn't give up on Martha. She was so fine underneath, he wanted her to get rid of her external "pickiness."

Now, a slightly different group of modern women could belong with Martha in this second scene. This group would be made up of women who have been close to the Lord, who perhaps have vowed to stop being so fussy and bossy. Yet, when an occasion arises that frustrates and annoys them, they just can't help from blaming someone else. They, like Martha, need a second teaching from the Lord. Too, they again like Martha may object to outward discomfort and inconvenience when they are about to behold a miracle.

They perhaps will hear, if they listen well, Jesus saying to them, "Didn't I tell you that if you could believe, you would see the glory of God?"

Hear carefully, women. Pray God you hear this sweet plea!

10

The Woman with a Spirit
of Infirmity

A Woman Bowed Down

Luke 13:10-17

And he was teaching in one of the synagogues on the sabbath.

And, behold, there was a woman which had a spirit of infirmity eighteen years, and was bowed together, and could in no wise lift up herself.

And when Jesus saw her, he called her to him, and said unto her, Woman, thou art loosed from thine infirmity.

And he laid his hands on her: and immediately she was made straight, and glorified God.

And the ruler of the synagogue answered with indignation, because that Jesus had healed on the sabbath day, and said unto the people, There are six days in which men ought to work: in them therefore come and be healed, and not on the sabbath day.

The Lord then answered him, and said, Thou hypocrite, doth not each one of you on the sabbath loose his ox or his ass from the stall, and lead him away to watering?

And ought not this woman, being a daughter of Abraham, whom Satan hath bound, lo, these eighteen years, be loosed from this bond on the sabbath day?

And when he had said these things, all his adversaries were ashamed: and all the people rejoiced for all the glorious things that were done by him.

Another woman heard the words of Jesus directed to her personally in an indefinite time and an uncertain place.

All we know for sure is: she was in one of the synagogues on the sabbath. From the other events preceding this miracle, we believe that this incident occurred during the Perean ministry of Jesus. Since the phrase, "one of the synagogues," is used, this particular place of worship must have been in a small town.

Luke is the only one of the Gospel writers who relates this story. Perhaps his interest here is singular because he is a physician and was most interested in every aspect of the disease and its cure, physically as well as spiritually.

Jesus was in the synagogue on this sabbath day as was his custom. Someone else special was also in the synagogue that day!

There was this woman with a "spirit of infirmity" which had lasted for eighteen years. She was so crooked, deformed, and bent over that she could not look up. Her condition seemed to be partly physical and partly mental. She may have grown so used to being unable to lift herself up, that she permitted her weakness to paralyze her efforts.

Christ described her as "whom Satan hath

bound" which would mean more than just physical affliction. Perhaps permitted power of evil made her like that.

This poor sufferer was of Abraham's faith. One of that faith came to worship no matter what the cost. What an effort it must have been for her to attend. But crippled though she was, crooked of body so that she could not see the teachers of the synagogue, yet she was there!

But what if she had not gone that day? What if on that one sabbath day she had decided that the effort to go was not worthwhile?

She came to be taught, but Christ gave her bodily relief. The house of God turned out to be the best possible place for a sufferer.

We are not aware if she had heard of or if she had seen Jesus before that miracle day.

Her case was different from many others involving miracles. She did not have to ask for healing.

It was also different from many other healings because Jesus didn't ask about her faith. He probably read it in her heart.

Jesus simply saw her as she was and extended his mercy to her. He must have sensed her devotion and faith through her coming to the synagogue in her pitiful condition.

When he called her to him, he said, "Thou art loosed." This was the only time he used this phrase in relation to disease. As soon as Jesus put his hands on her, she became straight.

There is another strange omission in this

healing scene. Jesus did not say, as he does on so many occasions, "Thy sins are forgiven thee."

This healing represents the power of the Savior against human misery. The Savior can deliver anyone from suffering. The immediate cure shows his divine power.

God can relieve us even after long affliction. This poor woman couldn't lift herself up but Christ could.

This divine power is just the opposite of human power as described in Ecclesiastes 7:13:

Consider the work of God: for who can make that straight, which he hath made crooked?

As soon as the woman was healed, as soon as her crooked body was made straight, she glorified God. Her instant gratitude to God was proof of her devotion.

If we had never before read about this miracle, our hearts would still be filled with joy that the woman managed with great difficulty to attend the synagogue, was noticed by Christ, was healed instantly, and glorified God in praise and gratitude.

But now came a flaw—the ruler of the synagogue didn't rejoice. He was indignant at the honor done in the synagogue. He failed to grasp the wonder of eighteen years' suffering and humiliation wiped away in the twinkling of an eye. He was "picky." All he saw was the breaking of the sabbath. He became wrathful because he thought the sabbath had been profaned.

It seems he didn't dare speak directly to Jesus or even to the newly liberated woman. He addressed the crowd in general. He spoke of six days for work, inferring that he would have preferred the woeful sufferer to have waited another day in her misery before she could have been healed.

This ruler was an example of how enemies of God's work can put on the look of piety. But Jesus didn't let his remark pass without an answer. In fact, Jesus answered him with extreme severity, reprimanding the hypocrisy of the Pharisees until they were ashamed.

Jesus reminded them that the Jews were permitted to loose their cattle for watering on the sabbath. He then asked, why shouldn't this woman be loosed from her bonds on the sabbath likewise? One rule the Jews held was that a physician could treat someone on the sabbath in an emergency, but not one who had a chronic disease. Jesus brought forth the belief that love and necessity know no law. The Lord claimed power over the sabbath.

As this anticlimax of the miracle is about to leave a bad taste in our mouths, a happier scene set in again. We learn that all the people there rejoiced for all the glorious works done by Jesus. They perhaps were particularly joyful because Jesus didn't labor in vain.

They learned then, as we do now, that we

must wait for the Lord, sometimes longer than we think we can, the moment of healing. We recognize as they must have, that spirits bound with infirmity look down instead of up to Christ. Christ alone can loose us from chains.

Now, why was this woman one of the privileged few to converse with Jesus in his ministry along the Galilean shores?

More than anything else, Jesus knew the devotion and loyalty of this woman, or else she wouldn't have come out on the sabbath in her sad state.

Also, he must have thought that she had waited long enough. He was there with her. His heart must have been deeply touched by all of those long, suffering, dragging, tormenting years she had endured.

He might have thought of her as a perfect example of being loosed from her bonds by the touch of the Master. Too, since he didn't say that her sins were forgiven, she must have been an especially good person.

Where is this woman today among the sisters of the world? She lives in every feminine heart that is bowed down with anguish, either physical or spiritual. She lives in every soul that is bound by something negative which causes one to look down instead of up.

She dwells in the mind of any woman who confesses that her life is crooked, but longs to have it straight.

If anyone in this category will keep loyalty and devotion uppermost, they also, above the hurt and sorrow, can hear the voice of Jesus saying: "Thou art loosed."

He will lay his hands on you, too. Then for the straightening, you can instantly glorify God.

11

Salome—Mother of James and John

A Woman Wrongly Motivated

Matthew 20:20-28

Then came to him the mother of Zebedee's children with her sons, worshipping him, and desiring a certain thing of him.

And he said unto her, What wilt thou? She saith unto him, Grant that these my two sons may sit, the one on thy right hand, and the other on the left, in thy kingdom.

But Jesus answered and said, Ye know not what ye ask. Are ye able to drink of the cup that I shall drink of, and to be baptized with the baptism that I am baptized with? They say unto him, We are able.

And he saith unto them, Ye shall drink indeed of my cup, and be baptized with the baptism that I am baptized with: but to sit on my right hand, and on my left, is not mine to give, but it shall be given to them for whom it is prepared of my Father.

And when the ten heard it, they were moved with indignation against the two brethren.

But Jesus called them unto him, and said, Ye know that the princes of the Gentiles exercise dominion over them, and they that are great exercise authority upon them.

But it shall not be so among you: but whosoever will be great among you, let him be your minister;

And whosoever will be chief among you, let him be your servant:

Even as the Son of man came not to be ministered unto, but to minister, and to give his life a ransom for many. (See also Mark 10:35-45.)

It is not surprising that Jesus would choose a mother as one with whom he would speak. This particular mother is in addition to his own mother, Mary.

Late in the Perean ministry of Jesus, Salome, the wife of Zebedee, appeared.

It is good that we can read of this conversation. Sometimes we tend to think of Jesus' concern as related only to the poor, the wretched, the miserable, the downbeat flow of humanity. We are thus limiting his love and compassion. For he also had a definite, loving message for the rich and the prominent. No fortunate or unfortunate person lies beyond his circle of care and vigilance.

Salome's husband was a fisherman on the Sea of Galilee. Evidently he was wealthy, for we learn in Mark 1:19-20 that his hired servants were with him.

Salome is the mother of the apostles James and John, called the "sons of thunder" due to their impetuous nature.

So we learn that Jesus took time to talk with a wealthy woman. Peter, James, and John are the three apostles who seem to have distinguished themselves and are often called "the inner circle." These three were the only followers of the Lord who saw Jesus raise the daughter of Jairus from the dead, witnessed the miracle of the transfiguration, and later went with Jesus apart from the others in the garden of Gethsemane just before his trial and crucifixion.

Furthermore, John, we learn later, was known to the High Priest. John referred to himself as the disciple "whom Jesus loved" because of the special love the Savior held for him. This was the disciple to whom Jesus on the cross entrusted the responsibility of looking after his mother, Mary. This is the one who ran with Peter to the tomb on the resurrection day. It was this John who wrote the three epistles bearing his name, the Gospel of John, and the Book of Revelation.

Her sons had a further distinction. James was the first apostle to die for Jesus. John was the last we have an account of, banished in exile to the Isle of Patmos. So here is Jesus speaking to a woman wealthy, prominent, and blessed with two most distinguished sons.

But a selfish attitude introduces her in the Bible narrative. She talked with Jesus during the critical time when he was trying to impress on his disciples that he was going down to Jerusalem to die. But what are the disciples thinking about first of all? Or what is foremost in the mind of this mother? Either these two disciples, or Salome, or maybe all three in this family were still thinking of rank and precedence in whatever kingdom Jesus was speaking about.

Here indeed was a woman of dual nature. She had to be daring. She had the audacity to approach Jesus when he had taken the twelve to give them final words about his crucifixion and resurrection. She dared to interrupt this soul-baring counseling time.

She was ardent in her procedure. She brought her sons with her as she worshiped Jesus. She was their advocate or their tool in this request. She did acknowledge Jesus as the Messiah. She followed her worship by asking a certain request of the Lord. It seems that she must have asked him to grant her a favor without stating a direct request.

How often we impose upon our friends when we say, "Promise me you will do something for me," before we reveal what the promise entails. This is not fair or logical.

Jesus didn't fall into Salome's trap. He promised her nothing without full knowledge of her specific request.

So the words he actually spoke to her and to no one else in the group formed the haunting question: "What wilt thou?"

In other words, Jesus wanted her to speak plainly about what she wanted.

Then she revealed her ambition. She actual-

ly had the gall to ask Jesus to let her sons,
James and John, sit one on the right hand and
one on the left in his kingdom.

It seems that in her ambition she forgot all
about Peter who had always been included
with them in their special experiences with
Jesus.

I wonder if she looked past Peter in her
eagerness to get to Jesus with James and
John. Perhaps impetuous Peter cast impatient
glances at her as she might have rudely
brushed against him, pressing through to
Jesus.

When she made that brazen request, she was
acting according to the custom of the East. For
the highest honor was to sit on the right, and
the next was to sit on the left. We will recall
that this is the way Jonathan and Abner were
seated by King Saul.

Jesus apparently spared her embarrassment by giving his answer to her plea, not directly to her but to the disciples as well.

First of all, Jesus replied, "Ye know not what
ye ask." The Lord continued to reply in mercy
and compassion toward what can only be
called their ignorance. He explained that the
highest places go to those who deserve them;
that only those who are dedicated in devotion
will be able to identify with him and his suffering. Christ declared that those who attain
higher positions must suffer and serve; that
discipleship is a costly pathway.

Her question caused dissension among the twelve, for ambition and jealousy frequently evoke each other. The other ten disciples became angry. They probably would have asked the same question themselves. Could it be they were disturbed because they were not the first to seek favoritism?

So for their anger they were no better than James and John and Salome. But Jesus got in the last words as he clarified his new concept of greatness.

Whosoever will be great among you, let him be your minister.

And whosoever of you will be the chiefest, shall be servant of all.

Now, why did this woman, among the chosen twelve, get to talk with Jesus?

Was it her wealth?

Was it her prominence?

Was it because she had two distinguished sons?

Was it her courage?

Was it because she had come worshiping Jesus?

Was it her ardor?

Was it because of her ambition for her sons?

Was it because she was being used as a tool by her sons?

Surely for none of these reasons did Jesus take time, prior to his triumphal entry into Jerusalem, to talk with a self-seeking woman.

Perhaps his conversation with her, which was broad enough in scope to include the twelve disciples, occurred to teach the lesson that they had used his words of comfort for the wrong purpose. They had abused his message of solace by being puffed up.

Does Salome live and breathe and become a reflection of many women in this century? There are countless women who do not hesitate to interrupt private, sacred groups to seek favors for themselves or their children.

Whether Salome dragged her sons into this scene of boldly seeking honor, or whether she was their instrument to cover up for them, we do not rightly know. In either case, there are women today who push their children in getting ahead or they let their children use them in this selfish manner.

I recall on one occasion when my husband was principal of the local high school that a prominent woman called to ask if her daughter, a senior-class member, might sing at the graduation services. We never knew if the daughter had her do this or whether it was the mother's idea. Anway, the daughter had a place of prominence on the program and on stage that special night. The jealous glances of some of the class members who could sing equally as well were quite visible that festive evening.

Salome plainly ignored Peter from the usual grouping with James and John. Many women today pass by good friends to get their children to the top.

So many modern mothers, like Salome, don't know what they are asking for their children. I have known mothers who prayed that their sons might enter certain professions of high esteem. These very professions presented so many temptations that only wretchedness and misery resulted.

The saving grace of this scene is that Salome, above all her petty selfishness, did worship Jesus.

Maybe the women of today in this category—of selfish seeking, pushing into sacred groups, demanding attention, ignoring others of equal rank—may still, if they truly worship at the feet of Jesus, learn the age-old truth. "Whosoever will be chief among you, let him be your servant."

Perhaps Salome learned the lesson of service, for we read in Matthew 27:55-56: "And many women were there beholding afar off, which followed Jesus from Galilee, ministering unto him: Among which was Mary Magdalene, and Mary the mother of James and Joses, and the mother of Zebedee's children."

And note Mark 16:1-8:

And when the sabbath was past, Mary Magdalene, and Mary the mother of James, and Salome, had bought sweet spices that they might come and anoint him.

And very early in the morning the first day of the week, they came unto the sepulchre at the rising of the sun. And they said among themselves, Who shall roll us away the stone from the door of the sepulchre? And when they looked, they saw that the stone was rolled away: for it was very great.

And entering into the sepulchre, they saw a young man sitting on the right side, clothed in a long, white garment; and they were affrighted.

And he saith unto them, Be not affrighted: Ye seek Jesus of Nazareth, which was crucified: he is risen; he is not here: behold the place where they laid him.

But go your way, tell his disciples and Peter that he goeth before you into Galilee: there shall ye see him, as he said unto you.

And they went out quickly, and fled from the sepulchre; for they trembled and were amazed: neither said they any thing to any man; for they were afraid.

12
Mary Magdalene

A Most Favored One

Mark 16:9-11

Now when Jesus was risen, early the first day of the week, he appeared first to Mary Magdalene, out of whom he had cast seven devils.

And she went and told them that had been with him, as they mourned and wept.

And they, when they had heard that he was alive, and had been seen of her, believed not.

John 20:1-18

The first day of the week cometh Mary Magdalene early, when it was yet dark, unto the sepulchre, and seeth the stone taken away from the sepulchre.

Then she runneth, and cometh to Simon Peter, and to the other disciple, whom Jesus loved, and saith unto them, They have taken away the Lord out of the sepulchre, and we know not where they have laid him.

Peter therefore went forth, and that other disciple, and came to the sepulchre.

So they ran both together: and the other disciple did outrun Peter, and came first to the sepulchre.

And he stooping down, and looking in, saw the linen clothes lying; yet went he not in.

Then cometh Simon Peter following him, and went into the sepulchre, and seeth the linen clothes lie,

And the napkin, that was about his head, not lying with the linen clothes, but wrapped together in a place by itself.

Then went in also that other disciple, which came first to the sepulchre, and he saw, and believed.

For as yet they knew not the scripture, that he must rise again from the dead.

Then the disciples went away again unto their own home.

But Mary stood without at the sepulchre weeping: and as she wept, she stooped down, and looked into the sepulchre,

And seeth two angels in white sitting, the one at the head, and the other at the feet, where the body of Jesus had lain.

And they say unto her, Woman, why weepest thou? She saith unto them, Because they have taken away my Lord, and I know not where they have laid him.

And when she had thus said, she turned herself back, and saw Jesus standing, and knew not that it was Jesus.

Jesus saith unto her, Woman, why weepest thou? whom seekest thou? She, supposing him to be the gardener, saith unto him, Sir, if thou have borne him hence, tell me where thou hast laid him, and I will take him away.

Jesus saith unto her, Mary. She turned herself, and saith unto him, Rabboni; which is to say, Master.

Jesus saith unto her, Touch me not; for I am not yet ascended to my Father: but go to my brethren, and say unto them, I ascend unto my Father, and your Father; and to my God, and your God.

Mary Magdalene came and told the disciples that she had seen the Lord, and that he had spoken these things unto her.

Of all the scenes in which Jesus talked with women, this one is without question the most joyous in its outcome!

Who wouldn't long to be the first person to whom the resurrected Lord appeared, let alone talked with also?

This encounter on the first day of the week should be known thereafter as resurrection day.

John in his Gospel does not mention the other women as being with Mary Magdalene. Mary came to the sepulchre as soon as she could while it was still dark. That was like her to do that. She had been at the cross. She was the last to leave in humiliation and the first to know the exaltation of his resurrection.

Magdalene means native of Magdala, which lay on the southwest coast of Galilee.

Mary had observed the Lord's burial and on the third day went to the sepulchre to anoint his body. Maybe she even thought she could steal him away.

When Mary saw the stone rolled away from the sepulchre, we naturally suppose before we read further that she would know the Lord had arisen. But, no, she thought he had been stolen away.

Notice her concern for the disciples. As soon

as she saw the stone rolled away, she ran to tell Simon Peter and John. We can envision her breathless as she reached them and perhaps tearfully bursting forth. "They have taken away the Lord out of the sepulchre, and we know not where they have laid him."

When Mary used the pronoun "we," we think this may mean that she included the other women with her, the different women mentioned by name in the other Gospels.

Then Peter and John rushed to the sepulchre. When they saw the linen clothes lying there, first Peter and then John went into the sepulchre. After looking about, Peter and John returned home.

But Mary, who had apparently gone back to the sepulchre with Peter and John, or at least shortly thereafter, did not return home with them.

She stayed at the sepulchre, weeping. She did not seem afraid. For love of Christ takes away fear, and Mary Magdalene loved much.

When Mary looked into the sepulchre, she saw two angels in white, one at the head and the other at the foot of the bier where Jesus had lain.

The angels asked her why she was weeping. Mary did not seem at all alarmed at their presence. She replied in a logical manner, that they (we don't exactly know whom she supposed) had taken away her Lord. She didn't know where they had laid him.

We have a glimpse of her great love when she did not say "the" Lord, but claimed him for her very own, "my" Lord.

After that, she turned herself back. Perhaps when the angels saw Jesus, their expression caused her to look back.

She saw Jesus standing there, but she didn't recognize him.

The first words the risen Christ spoke now reverberate across the pages of history. It is not surprising that his first words were of concern.

"Woman, why weepest thou? whom seekest thou?"

We wonder of course why Mary did not recognize Jesus. Probably it was because of her great grief and her continuous weeping. She may have only halfway seen him because her head was bowed in sorrow.

She supposed him to be the gardener because he was so friendly. She replied to him with an address of courtesy, "Sir." Her intense longing to find Jesus was expressed again as she said, "If thou have borne him hence, tell me where thou hast laid him, and I will take him away."

Then Jesus called her name. It must have been with deep kindness and tenderness. "Mary."

How wonderful that Christ knows us by name too!

This one word as he speaks her name broke

through her grieving and despair. His triumph began with a simple dialogue. Sometimes Christ has to show *us* to *ourselves*.

When Mary heard her name, she knew him. She turned and called out: "Rabboni." The term "Rabboni" shows more honor than the term "Rabbi."

Then Jesus had a special message for her: "Touch me not."

His words were to end the past, and to look for the joys of the future.

His resurrection was looking toward the ascension. "For I am not yet ascended to my Father."

Then Jesus appointed her to go tell the others of his resurrection and his approaching ascension.

How marvelous to understand that this Mary, out of whom the Lord had cast seven devils, was now favored to carry the message of the risen Christ to the disciples.

This was part of her reward for her constancy. She was the last to leave Christ on crucifixion day and the first to go to his sepulchre.

Mary Magdalene went to the disciples with a faithful report of what she had seen and heard. Peter and John had left her at the sepulchre, but now she went to them.

Mary Magdalene was fit in spirit to be the first to see the risen Lord and to tell the disciples of his resurrection. People try to malign her, but she will be remembered as the first one to witness the resurrection.

There is no evidence that she had been evil, only that she was ill, perhaps mentally ill. Jesus had cured her. She had made a comeback to health. She expressed her appreciation in faithful service. For she had followed Jesus as he preached. She was one of his most devoted disciples during his early Galilean ministry. She ministered to him of her substance.

And now the risen Savior had revealed himself first of all to this poor woman. Mary, much forgiven, was sent to comfort weeping Peter, and the others. The Lord truly blesses those who are not ashamed of him. For her to be sent as the Lord's messenger was a signal honor.

Mary Magdalene had made the mistake of looking for a dead Christ, when already he was a risen Christ. Actually, Mary did not find Christ—he found her.

She was seeing him, yet she did not recognize him. But like Mary Magdalene, the closer we are to Christ, the sooner we can expect to see him.

It comes through rather clearly why Jesus must have chosen Mary Magdalene as one of the few women with whom he had a recorded conversation.

She was grateful for the Lord's blessings which she had experienced. She enjoyed active gratitude, not mere lip service. For she followed him and served him as he preached. She could not bear to leave him on the cross. Her loyalty was further exhibited by her being so eager to be at the sepulchre on the third day for the anointing.

She had courage, for she came perhaps alone into the darkness to the sepulchre.

She not only loved the Lord, but she loved humankind. For she ran to tell Peter and John when she saw the stone rolled away from the sepulchre.

Mary Magdalene was not one to forsake her purpose. She wanted to know where Christ was when he was not in the grave. She stayed there weeping, even when Peter and John had deserted.

She was not easily disturbed. She was very calm when she saw two angels where Jesus had laid.

She was humble, for she apparently thought nothing about the angels honoring her with their questions.

She was sensitive for she appeared in anguish when she did not know where the Lord was.

She used every opportunity for help. When Jesus, whom she supposed to be the gardener, spoke to her, she asked him also to tell her where Jesus was.

She was reverent. When she recognized Jesus, she immediately called him, "Rabboni."

She was understanding. When Jesus explained that their relationship was now different from how it was before his resurrection, she did not question him.

She was obedient. When Jesus told her to go as a messenger of joy to the disciples, she went immediately.

She was not vindictive. Peter and John left her alone at the sepulchre. There is no evidence that they tried to console her. There is no suggestion that they would believe her story, but she ran to the disciples and told them all that had happened to her.

How does Mary Magdalene fit into the picture of modern women?

What kind of women today could be called Mary Magdalenes?

Any woman belongs in this blessed group who has had a serious illness and through prayer has regained her health, if she has given back to the Lord grateful service in return.

Any woman belongs in this group who lives so close to the Lord that she has the staying power of loyalty, the courage to go along dark pathways of life alone.

Today's women also belong in this group who want to share the news of the Lord with others.

Any woman also fits here who, though filled with sorrow, will continue to search for the Lord. When others give up, these women hold on tenaciously.

Any woman belongs here who humbly accepts being singled out for special blessings.

Women are Mary Magdalenes if they are reverent, obedient, and sharing.

The women of Mary Magdalene's group are among the choicest!